NOT IN THE SCRIPT

Elizabeth Green

Text copyright © 2020 by Elizabeth Green

ISBN 979-8-6691-9705-6

Printed in the U.S.A.

10 9 8 7 6 5 4 3 2 1

Dedicated to all my family
'Here's another fine mess you've gotten us into.'
Also my 'chosen' family Jake Stackhouse,
Nubia, Ludovica and Rita in SF.
Oh and my 'wicked sister' Lyndsey! Your turn girl!

Thank you to my dear friend Richard who, whilst doing a hugely competent 'polish', kept up my spirits from across the Atlantic.

A LIGHTBULB MOMENT

CHAPTER 1

I was brought up in a cold climate, and I don't mean the weather.

There were no role models in my house. Well, not any that I cared to learn from. I'm the opposite of my mother, I'm warm and loving, more like the Greens of my father's family. But then we didn't 'do' family, my mother didn't like family!

I'm standing in the luscious back garden of my large Edwardian house in North London. It had just been expensively replanted by Andy and Nili, my landscape gardeners.

It was the day before my wedding anniversary. I knew it was a farce and I chose my words carefully.

'How would you like to mark the occasion?' I asked David tentatively.

'Celebrate? Why would I want to celebrate with you?' my soon-to-be ex-husband exploded.

I recently used the expression 'suicidally optimistic'. I had been in that state for years.

This was the lightbulb moment.

In the moment I'm not quite sure what I said. Something like:

'You know, I think I'm done here, I'd like a divorce'

Sharp intake of breath followed, the 'D' word dropped like a bomb, after all, it had been hovering in the wind for so many years.

'Yes, let's not do this any more.'

I'd paid my dues, stayed together for the sake of the kids. They knew what was going on and nothing was going to surprise them.

We had come full circle: all the qualities he had liked in me, admired in me, were now the things he hated. I won't use the word 'love'. I'm not sure we did, love each other, I was never 'in love' with him.

Didn't feel brave at this moment, but found out later divorce is not for the faint-hearted. It was a strange moment when I finally said what had been on my mind for so long.

Anthony was staying for the weekend. He was doing a project with David, using his silky golden DJ tones. Anthony and I had history, chemistry even, had spent a lusty weekend together as part of his 'best man' duties at Bella's wedding, long before I was married.

I'd liked him, liked him a lot. But then I always liked anyone who seemed to show even a morsel of interest in me. A disease? An impediment? I'm a love-starved woman.

My family? I was brought up in middle-class neglect. Harder to spot when it's all on the inside, but no less painful than broken shoes, or all sharing one bedroom, even one bed. Yes, I had a big house, food, private school, nannies and absent parents, physically and mentally.

But no love! Did I need love if I had all the other stuff? I should just get on with things and be grateful, as was pointed out to me later in life by my mother.

Yes, she'd had a hard upbringing, tough mothering. So she did what she knew to do, she did not show her emotions, she was the odd one out so her brother Harold told me.

Even though I was educated and 'smart', I remember the day I got married. I took a breath, and finally as we stood at the register office, said to myself: 'made it'. Then I kept my commitment, for 23 years, until that moment in the garden.

I went into the house, Anthony was inside. I think he knew what was going on. The dogs were sniffling around our ankles.

'Shall we go to the woods and walk the dogs?' he asked.

'Sure.'

I had seen Anthony in the years since our dalliance. Bella's marriage ended and he had been in a relationship with Bella, keeping things close to home, we had gone out on double dates, me and David and Bella and Anthony.

In the torture and misery of my marriage I never noticed Anthony's little extra attentions. In the restaurant he would push my chair in, and his hand would linger, longer than needed on my back, as he pushed it into the table. When Bella fell asleep on the sofa after Christmas lunch, he sat next to me, and laughed at all my jokes and put his arm round my shoulder.

So naturally on these dates Anthony and David had started talking about work, that's what men do, anything except talk about feelings, emotions, real life. So a project was born.

I put the lead on the dogs, my two crazy pugs.

'Here, one each, let's walk.'

The woods were down the road, round the corner. There was undergrowth and brush and mud like a real wood, just in the London suburbs. The dogs liked it.

'So how are you dear Elizabeth?' Anthony seemed concerned.

'Truthfully, I'm in shock. I heard the words come out of my mouth. I feel daunted but better.'

'It'll be OK, I'm here.'

He reached out to hug me and I snuggled in, glad of the warmth and comfort. He took my face and tilted it up to look at his, and bent down and kissed me. On the mouth.

'Anthony, what are you doing?'

'Just letting you know I'm here for you. Always have been.'

Wow. My whole future flashed before me.

'Let's get back.'

'Yes let's. We can speak when I'm back in Manchester.'

We went back to the house, kids and chaos. 'Anthony and I' got lost in the confusion and soon he left for the trek back up North.

'Bye Anthony.' I hugged him on the doorstep, he held me close just a little tighter and longer than usual, but in the chaos of someone leaving, no-one noticed.

Next day he texted me, and I texted back, and then we were in it.

David and I, meanwhile, went to bed. I slept as far over on my side as possible, thank God the bed was huge. I'm surprised I didn't fall out, but luckily he had stopped reaching for me.

But now I'd used the 'D' word, in my mind I was divorced and the pretense was over, just the nuts and bolts needed sorting out. The house, the money, I didn't have much, the three kids and who would live where and, apparently, I was keeping the dogs!

Anthony and I spoke every night now all the longing and the lust was on the table.

'Do you remember that Christmas when I was there with Bella, having lunch?'

'I do.'

'And I had my arm round you on the sofa, well really all I wanted to do was take you into the corner and fuck you.'

'OK.'

'Because I've been in love with you since we were together all those years ago. Still am.'

Deep intake of breathe, mine. Oh my God, what would it feel like to be wanted again, in the bedroom and outside.

'We should go away together,' he suggested.

'We should, far away, to the sunshine. I'm going to talk to Cathy my friend and personal trainer, see what she comes up with. She knows exotic and, unfortunately, expensive places.'

I tucked myself away in the bedroom, to watch TV and find a wonderful place to lie in the sun and feel pampered.

Cathy came up with a plan. Anguilla, yes not just Antigua but on to the smaller island, exotic and further away. No-one would ever know or find us.

'I'm going away with Cathy and her mother for a couple of weeks.'

No-one was listening, no one seemed bothered. Kept my tracks covered. So I thought!

This is not going to be a fucking adventure story, you know, Enid Blyton. This is my life, how I felt, what went on, what went wrong. About love, life and disappointment!

So before two weeks in the Caribbean we decided to have an English weekend away.

We chose Stratford upon Avon, culture, and candour and whatever else happened.

'David' - I hated using his name…. 'David I'm going away for the weekend with cousin Esther. Back Sunday.'

'OK' he says grudgingly. We're at the point of almost no talk, can't bear to, can't bear each other. Would that it would be over, but it's going to take longer than that.

And then we're driving to Stratford. The green Toyota Rav 4 still has legs, or would wheels sound more appropriate? He has the map. I'm the driver.

I've done my research, we have a country hotel, big double bed for two.

That moment when you get into bed with someone who cares, who likes you, who wants to hold you and love you, I had forgotten how that felt. That warmth, I'm young again, we're lusty and loving, Anthony, who's now carrying a few extra pounds, not as nimble as he was, but my heart is singing. I'm a couple again, part of a pair. He stretches out his arms as I sigh and he pulls me in close. That was my one thought about getting divorced. What will happen? Will I ever have sex again? Seems I will. I am and it's not bad either, just need to learn each other's rhythm.

First morning we wake up to newspapers full of my brother. My brother's knighthood, what a star, my mother is kvelling! So proud.

Us, we're just wandering amongst the ordinary people. We see a Shakespeare play as we're in his birthplace - Shakespeare in Japanese, nearly impenetrable in English, in Japanese.....impossible. They're using ribbons of red for blood, strange but effective. We leave at the intermission.

NEW LOVE, DOESN'T LAST

CHAPTER 2

So with some secrecy, I booked for Anthony and me to go to Anguilla. This meant a long plane ride to Antigua and then a small prop plane to Anguilla where the pace of life was slow and languid, like the water in the infinity pool outside our villa.

I think I was more interested in impressing Jane, Cathy's mum, than Anthony. And Jane took to tutoring Anthony in the ways of life, and enlightenment and heart so he was much taken up with her. Cathy just worshipped the sun, topless in our pool, and practically bottomless as well.

We went inland a few times, between mother and daughter arguments about who should wash up, fold the laundry and put the magazines back in the rack. We had a maid, thank God, and Anthony was our designated driver. We had hired a car.

There was a beautiful resort nearby and we had dinner with our feet swooshing in the sand. It was so peaceful and mostly loving, many hugs and tentative love-making with Anthony. He was tentative, I was impatient and starved.

Then the phone calls started. David had been in my computer and found the one thing that mentioned Anthony's name, a receipt for the car hire, and the barrage started and continued, and continued.

Turns out he'd called my mother, my family, anyone who would listen. He bumped into Bella in the local supermarket and broke down in the aisle telling her about Anthony's treachery. But I had made sure he was done with her before embarking on anything, and I had told my sister-in-law about Anthony. I'm a smart girl.

Last day, we're facing a long journey home. No liquids allowed on flights, new rule established since our departure, a new security measure. They confiscated Cathy's new very expensive designer lipstick so she sat in a fury.

Now I arrived home to hell let loose.

My soon to-be ex-husband had just been released from hospital. Seems he'd decided to try and gas himself in the family car, whilst sitting on the driveway.

Idiot. The ignition had a switch to turn off the engine when gases got dangerous, the point at which my two youngest kids had found him. Georgia and Jacob had to call an ambulance and he was taken to the local A&E department, on suicide watch.

I didn't know what to be more furious about - his futile attempt to end it all, or his doing it in front of the kids and letting them be the grownups and look after him.

'What were you thinking?'

'I want to be with you, I'll change, I will,' he said tearfully.

'You won't, you don't like me. You haven't liked me for many years. It's not going to happen.'

So many times I would have given in, like the people pleaser I'd become over the years.

'Ruth told me what you said to her. You told her you'd absolutely hated me for the past two years. I don't think you're going to come back from that.'

He stopped sobbing long enough to tell me I should move my things downstairs and sleep in Simon's room, my eldest son who'd gone to university.

'But that's not going to work. All my stuff is up here.'

'Too bad, you should have thought of that.'

Life carried on. We spoke to our respective lawyers. Mine told me 'Don't argue with him. Don't get into it with him. Just maintain the peace.'

So I did.

Now he knew about Anthony, I could go and see him when he

came to London. We would stay in nearby Barnet with friends.

One night, I'm in Barnet at Greg's seeing Anthony. They're rather tickled that Anthony has met someone at long last.

The phone rings. It's David.

'It's your turn to walk the dogs' he tells me.

'But I'm not there.'

'Well you should be and you should come home and do it.'

'No,' I say as I hang up. Never should have taken the call.

Two nights later he tries a new tactic to get me into an argument.

'Why do you keep running up the road to see him? I bet he's not as good in bed as me.'

WHAT! You kidding? Maybe not?

'Why would you say something like that?'

'Because you know you'll miss me, and want me, and you'll be sorry.'

No I won't! And no, I won't.

'Just leave it alone. It's not a competition, and anyway you don't want me.'

Hasn't got the balls to say the thing that's on his mind, that male thing, if he can't have me, then no-one else can either.

Anthony and I take a trip to the ballet at Sadler's Wells. to see his son, the son he hasn't seen for five years. He somehow found out he was performing and is hoping to grab him at the stage door and say something, anything, whatever it is you say after five years.

His ex had poisoned the boy against his father. Now I had to prep him for those maybe two precious minutes he might get to stake his claim, be eye to eye, I don't know … just tell him he's loved and missed.

Isn't that the only thing to say?

He can hardly sit through the ballet. We spot his son in the chorus from our seats so high up in the upper tier of the theatre. I'm not even quite sure which one he is, but I don't tell Anthony, he's stressed enough already.

As the last chorus crescendos I push him out to run down all the flights of stairs to the stage door. I take my time to let them have their private moment.

By the time I get there, they've spoken and his son has disappeared into the night.

'Was it OK?' I look at his tearful face and I know the answer already.

'Home, let's go home. I'm tired.'

Tired and emotional, and there are two young kids at Greg's house who may still be up with questions and bounces and giggles and demands.

Anthony goes back to Manchester to his little suburban house, and then he tells me he's in love with me. Just like that, and spoils things.

'I believe you. But I'm not ready, could you give me a moment or two? I'm not divorced yet.'

'I've been in love with you for the past two years.'

'What, all the time you were with Bella?'

'Yes, probably.'

'But she didn't know?'

'No, but she did say some horrible things about you, even though you were supposed to be best friends.'

I remembered back to those days in the playground, aged eight. The childish games we played back then. I think Bella and I were thrown together as the two left-outs. There was such a pecking order at my rather fancy private girls school. There were the popular girls who everyone wanted to be with, and then people like Bella and I. Marginal people drawn together for comfort, and then the pretense had continued on long into our 'adulthood'.

It was based on criticism, a form of communication my mother favored hugely. That's why Bella and my mother got on so well. One time after a holiday Bella and I had taken, we arrived home to find that the landlord of the flat we shared had not finished the promised renovations.

So we moved to my mother's house, no choice. But I found it intolerable and moved out, Bella stayed and buddied up with my mother. Best buddies.

Not me. Traitors, I was surrounded by traitors, so no, Anthony had not told me anything revolutionary and new.

'So all the time you were with her ... how can I trust you?'

'It's true. I love you.'

I have to leave Anthony to nurse his broken heart. We still speak but we're not planning a big future together.

David moves out. He tries to take the furniture. My brother has bought him out and he's found a flat to buy. I try to point out we need a table to sit at, a couch to lie on, and Simon is upset.

'Dad needs furniture, why can't he have it?'

'Simon, don't get involved. He will get furniture.'

He goes to the family store, and has free run. They seem more concerned about his well-being than mine. He has a table to eat at, a bed to sleep on, and a sofa from which to watch his new TV.

Then on Christmas Eve Anthony tells me he met someone. He's not going to wait for me, and that was that! Timing! Christmas Eve! I'm devastated but my daughter is wonderful and we stay in bed for a day and watch never ending 'Sex And The City'.

Even better than that, she walks the dogs, while I hide my head under the duvet.

It hurts for a while. It wasn't that I was so in love with him. Just in love with love and being loved.

I pass the hotel in North Finchley where we stayed the last time we were together. A poignant reminder? No, actually a rotten reminder.

We stay estranged for a long time, then he emails me, a mixture of compliments and insults, or I took it that way.

Hi, I'm in a relationship, and not a bad one. So why do I want to contact you? First of all I think you're sexy. A few Christmases back when Bella and I came to your place and I sat beside you on the couch, all I wanted to do was drag you somewhere and fuck you. Secondly I love your brain. No, not being patronizing....I love the way you think. Now the other side. You are without doubt the most manipulative and domineering female I have ever come across, you drive me to distraction. Also I have certain sexual foibles that I don't think would interest you. Bella may have been many things, but she was compliant ... in fact she enjoyed the role of a submissive ... ropes and all. So my love, I guess as I said on the phone earlier we aren't compatible. Oh but if we were!!!!

It's true E, I do love you (and have done since we met at Bella's wedding, you me and the maroon Morris Minor) and I want you to have the very best life. So go out there and have one! A xxx

You are right, Anthony. Not compatible.

THE PROMISED LAND

CHAPTER 3

So while Bella was living with my mother talking about sex and boys, the two of them giggling together I made other plans.

I had met Arthur Castle, and he had a quaint little flat in Highgate Village, with crooked floors and, I guess, crooked ceilings.

I lived in his spare bedroom and went to college. I had just been through a terrible moment in my life, an unwanted pregnancy, which I had filed away in my head somewhere, and it came back to haunt me during this time, but I just carried on and pretended to study.

Arthur worked in TV, glamorous and exciting, or so it looked to me. We were friends, kind of, and sat sometimes of an evening having a drink. I remember one evening when I was ill, he plied me with whisky, medicinal don't you know.

Angie and I, Arthur's girlfriend, were friends too. I was just a hippie lost girl, these were sophisticated people, except we shared Arthur.

On the nights when Angie didn't stay over, I was the next nearest choice. Obvious really, and no, we never told her.

One night Arthur and Angie came back with Roy. Roy was a playwright, at a successful period in his life, plays on TV, revered at that time for 'Scum,' a gritty play about Borstal, way outside the limits for the more modest broadcasting standards at this time in the world. Directed by Roy's friend Alan Clarke, much fêted and admired. We had watched it at home together.

Roy was from Nottingham, son of a miner; grey haired and gritty, brought up with none of the middle-class privileges from my life. Made him a better playwright than I could have been, suffering for your art.

'Hey this is Roy. Goodnight, Angie and I are going to bed.'

'Great, now what do we do?'

'Hey, shall we go to bed too?'

I'm startled. He's not my type, rough and northern, gaunt with grey hair. I'm snobby. Time to put aside my nice Jewish North London roots and prejudices.

'Sure.'

We climb the crooked stairs to a night of such delight. I realised in that moment, never judge a book by its cover. He was delicious in bed, there only for me, waiting for my satisfaction and fulfillment. Nothing like the 'boys' it seems I'd been fumbling with. He'd had a few drinks. Me, I came at this stone-cold sober. Every moment of it touched me. Wow! Who knew it could be like this....sex.

We slept, he in the unfamiliar bed, like babies. Next morning he gave me a gruff goodbye.

'See you again sometime luv, bye.'

Bye indeed.

Saturday night Roy's new play is on TV, Arthur is home to watch it then leaves soon after. I hate being on my own just like that. I know, I'm going to call Roy. It is long before the days of mobile phones, his wife might answer the house phone, but I think I remember him telling me she's away with their children, so I take a chance.

'Hello luv, how are you?'

'Oh the play was wonderful, Roy.'

'What are you doing luv?' he asked gruffly.

'Nothing, we just watched your play and Arthur has just gone out and left me here.'

'Do you want to come and visit me?'

'You're in Nottingham?'

'Yes, you can get the train, get off at Nottingham, get a cab and I'll leave the back door light on for you to find the way.'

'Are you alone? Where's your wife and kids?'

'They're away. Are you coming up?'

'OK' I'm nervous but never one to shy away from adventure.

It was late and I had to hurry to catch the last train. I put on my long embroidered Arab dress, sling my basket over my shoulder. The pub opposite cashes a cheque, thank God, and I'm on my way.

The taxi driver drops me in an unknown dark street with dim lighting. I suddenly realise this is a strange thing to do in the middle of the night. I'm a little fearful as I climb the back stairs to where a light is burning.

He was in bed. I just dropped my clothes on the floor and climbed into the big marital bed, where we made wild love. Liberating with no Arthur in the next room.

A couple of days pass, eating, sleeping and making love. Then as suddenly as I arrive, he sends me to get the train.

'Too clingy.' He pushes me away. I am, have been and will be, hard to change. But now I forgive myself for being that way.

'You should come and see me and Alan in London.'

'I will, thank you for looking after me.'

He's not good at thank yous, unfamiliar it seems. But I've promised to see them both in London.

Next night, Arthur comes home to find me on the phone to Alan Clarke. Clarkey. He's overhearing our conversation.

'I didn't know you knew him.' He's over curious.

'I don't, not yet.'

Alan is northern, different to Roy, warm and wonderful, and welcoming. I feel like I've known him a long, long time.

'Sweetheart, Roy told me all about you. Come over and visit me, I'm not far away. Don't bother to tell Arthur.

Alan welcomes me with open arms. We greet each other like long lost friends and lovers. He was tender where Roy was gruff, caring where Roy was abrupt, sweet where Roy was sour.

Alan's flat is something to behold. He lives in a basement in Islington where I think he's kept every milk bottle he's ever drunk from. But he was a genius, was this a mark of that genius? The bed was clean and wholesome; the rest of the place, truly, was horrible, to be avoided. We did laugh about it, and I got him some milk bottle crates. Many.

When Roy arrived, we just all went to bed together. I remember Alan would play Judy Collins in the background... 'I loved you in the morning, our kisses deep and warm, your hair upon the pillow like a sleepy golden storm, many loved before us, I know that we are not new, in city and in forest they smiled like me and you...' If I closed my eyes I could imagine I was in love and loved, he was tender and kind, and they weren't afraid of each other's bodies as we all took turns. It was warm and loving, and funny, we laughed and fucked and told stories, and hid from the world.

I met Alan's friends; playwrights and TV people. His landlord who lived upstairs with his family and kids seemed to want to be downstairs with us. We were fun, and crazy.

Roy and I found our new local pub, The King's Head. We became their best customers for a while. Arthur found out where I was, he never found out how I was, and we kept it that way.

I'm back in Islington as I remember those moments. The pub is still there, darling Alan sadly not. Some years later I found out he died of some horrible cancer. After holding goodbye parties round his bed, wish I'd gone. We met once at Dr. Sharma's, my homeopathic doctor's surgery. I was married with a small baby by then, he invited me round and sadly I said 'no, sweetheart, no.'

But before my firstborn there was an unwanted pregnancy that happened in Israel. I took a trip with my mother's two favourite girls from school who abandoned me on arrival. I was lost, did not know anyone there, boarded a bus just before the Sabbath, knowing I had better get situated before dusk or I would be stranded. All transport stopped for the Sabbath.

I was a little desperate as I struck up a conversation with the guy sitting next to me on the bus.

'Would you like to come to my kibbutz for Shabbat?'

'I would love to.' Of course, I knew what a kibbutz was. It was a communal way of life, or so I thought.

'That's very generous of you. Thank you.'

It was called Bet Kama, just south of Haifa, in the desert, where the air was dry, hot and dry.

I was scared, trepidatious, alone, did not phone home to tell them. I didn't think anyone would be bothered. My mother had given me money, sent me off happy to be rid of me, for once. This was my new adventure. What could happen?

I stayed six weeks, and a lot happened. I became well known and not so highly thought of around the kibbutz. I got to know quite a few members of the male population, the elders walked past me and shook their heads. There was Guy from Switzerland who strangled the chickens, a sweet Arab boy whose name I cannot recall, which is sad really because I think he was the father of my baby.

I picked apples going out on the tractor every morning at 5am to start before the sun got too hot. The scorpions were out at that hour too, heat didn't bother them. For your board and lodging they made you work. I climbed the trees on ladders with a big solid canvas container strapped in front of me to put the apples in. You couldn't just throw them in, it bruised them. These apples went into storage for six months before being put out for sale. Who knew? I didn't.

Anyway it was time to come home and live with my mother in

London and go back to college. The winter seemed cold after so much sunshine and my new boyfriend, Rob, a simple working class boy lived nearby up Highgate Hill, no buses ran up that hill, so we took to walking. It made me feel healthy and well, and not pregnant!

My periods, which had always been spotty, had disappeared and I needed to go and see a specialist, in Harley Street, the street it seemed of credible doctors. I didn't want to go with my mother. Luckily I was still friends with a friend of hers, so Irene Dula and I set off for the doctor. Irene had been wonderful to me a few years earlier.

My mother had to drive to my brother's Berkshire boarding school, unexpectedly, to collect him as he was about to be expelled. So she placed me under Irene's care for the weekend.

What a joy. What a nice lady, and how nice she thought I was too. Such a change from being told I was doing it wrong and being compared to others. I had a date that night, with Edward Landau, who took me out and treated me nicely and bought me dinner.

Luckily, because many years later, he turned out to be my brother's lawyer, and all we both had to report was a chaste kiss on the cheek as he brought me back to Irene's house.

Irene took me to the doctor in Harley Street where he gave me an internal examination, and did not discover I was six weeks pregnant. Nor did the pregnancy test I had taken show a positive result, and I was not sick, or fat, just my usual few pounds over. This esteemed doctor now confirmed a 'no' result.

'Come back in six months. Take these pills at the end of every month for three days, and your periods should come back.'

'Thank you very much.'

'I will see you in six months' time.'

'You will.'

'Any problems, telephone my secretary.'

We were ushered out of his office. It hardly looked like a conventional office. These were Regency houses, built for large families. The doctor's receptionist sat in what was once the dining room. I saw the doctor in what would have been the lounge for a large Victorian family, and the doctor conducted himself in the old fashioned manner of a Victorian gentleman. It was assumed while we spoke in hushed tones he knew his job, in my case he did not.

So I went away and took the pills, and did not get my periods. But I did take a few amphetamines to help me lose weight - injected through my tights by our family doctor, Eliot Lanford.

'This will make you lose weight wonderfully. Your appetite will disappear, you mark my words.'

He was right. I was so hyped up I could not sit down long enough to eat anything. So, although my belly increased, my hips were slim and svelte.

But I couldn't last six months and my mind was crazy by this time. I had a list of pros, and a list of cons. Why I could be pregnant, and why not? Luckily, new boyfriend Rob and I had a chaste relationship, not for want of trying on my part, but he had a Christian upbringing so sex before marriage was off the cards. Bugger me, couldn't make it happen. But apparently the Christian upbringing allowed everything but, so there were many messy episodes on top of the bed clothes.

Then I went back to the doctor with my mother, and he examined me and said, respecting my age; 'Is there anything that you would rather discuss privately with me first, not in front of your mother? For instance, if you were pregnant?'

My mouth fell slightly open. I didn't even look at her. Now he'd spilled the beans, he was going to tell me I was pregnant. What an arse.

'Yes, can I speak to you in private please?' As if private still existed.

'Yes, you can.'

My mother stepped outside the room and he said to me 'I've made a terrible mistake, you're six and a half months pregnant. If you want my help, I will help you to get rid of the baby. What would you like to do?'

What would I like to do? Reach over the desk and strike you. Scream, hide from my mother. She won't be an understanding mother.

'I don't want to have this baby. I have taken all kinds of medication whilst I was pregnant. I don't want to take the risk of something being wrong with the baby. Can you abort it please?'

I didn't, even in shock, mention that I had no idea who the father was, and if I was even half right this baby could be dark skinned. How would we pass that off?

My mother immediately said: 'You mustn't tell anybody. You can tell people you had an ovarian cyst. Then this can be over with.'

Compassionate and caring, showing her true colours as usual. Ever concerned with what people would think.

I'm in a private hospital in Tottenham Hale, It's secret. No-one knows. I'm going to be put to sleep and they will take the baby out. It's long ago when life was not so high tech, babies were not so viable, not so easily saved. So the doctor thinks he will be safe in his manoeuvres.

They don't bring me anaesthetic, and the nurse is left to explain. Explain that if the worthy doctor does an abortion at this late stage, the baby will be born alive and he will be culpable. So they break my waters, I barely know or understand what this is. After all, I'm 20. Why would I be studying childbirth? I'm just through childhood, still deciding what to be when I grow up, coming to grips with life, and the death of my father a few years before.

Incredible labour pains start, relentlessly, inevitably, until finally I'm ready to push.

'It won't hurt so much, the baby is small, not full term,' my caring mother had told me.

You are kidding. It couldn't hurt more than this. The baby comes out and is whisked away. They tell me nothing and the poor put upon nurse talks to me. The doctor stays far away.

'What did I have?'

'You had a boy.'

'What happened to him? What did they do?' She looks at me very sadly.

'They just did not start his life.'

Later, I discover the horrible truth. They put his body down the sluice. My heart is racing, I cannot ask anything more. My mother directs them to give me pills to stop my milk coming in.

Somehow, I'm detached from my body as I watched the birth, from a place on the ceiling in the corner of the room. I watched myself in disbelief and abandonment. I watched as if it happened to someone else. Sadly, it happened to me.

The doctor does his rounds.

Cheery voice: 'How's my patient today? Doing well? Jolly good.'

He didn't really want an answer, and I didn't really have one. A few days later I'm discharged, and then I go back to college. As if nothing happened. Rob is gone, back to find other fumblings, and a year later I'm living at Arthur's where I'm playing with fire again.

For many years I had this thought: maybe they had started his life, maybe I have a son running around somewhere in the world, who I don't know about.

THE MENTAL HOSPITAL,
A VERY SHORT STAY

CHAPTER 4

The flat I shared with Bella until the refurbishment that never got finished was in Westbourne Park. I lived there subsequently with Ann and her boyfriend.

She and all my brainy friends from school were at LSE (London School of Economics). I hadn't managed university. I went to a polytechnic, same studies, different environment.

I'd had my non-eventful 21st birthday there. No-one came and we barely celebrated. A few years later, my mother held a big party for my brother at the family home. Friends and family flocked, I was not invited, knew nothing about it. But the pictures of the night bear witness.

I didn't take it well, my 21st. I felt neglected and unloved. I invited people, problem was most of them said they couldn't come … or didn't want to, I never knew which.

I was living in Westbourne Park when I discovered I had contracted chicken pox. My mother decided when I was young that I should not be around any other kids who got sick. What a bad idea. Mumps aged 11 was painful and scary. Chicken pox aged 21 scary and unsightly. I sat on the bus to the doctor's with spots erupting, trying hard to cover my face. In those days you put Gentian Violet on the itching sores, so not only did you itch but you were a spectacle too. And then Ann caught it just before her finals, great idea mother. I was still with Ann and Geoff when I discovered I was pregnant.

I travelled every day to Highbury Fields to study at the polytechnic. I didn't have many friends so I had befriended one of the lecturers; Lyndsey and her small son Matthew. I would go over and eat and spend the night there. Lyndsey took me on holiday with them when they went to Greece to meet her Greek lover. Unofficial babysitter - and I'd paid my own ticket. Ripped off? The price of being wanted and needed was high! But I was grateful to be wanted, and Matthew was a sweet kid and I was allowed on some of the outings with them.

Octopus fishing, I recoiled in horror as all their arms pulsed on the deck of the small fishing boat.

Back in London, Lyndsey decided she didn't have time or inclination for me. I was so upset. Thinking, or not thinking straight, I thought to myself, I know I'll take all the pills she'd helped me get, then she'll want me, take notice, do something. It wasn't a serious life-ending attempt, more a cry for help.

I wanted to be admitted to the Maudsley hospital, near to Lyndsey's home in South London, and be looked after there. Instead, I ended up at Friern Barnet Mental hospital near where I lived in North London, an old Victorian work house, badly converted into a mental hospital.

It was the whole nine yards. More pills, morning meetings, lots of crazy people, really crazy people. Shaking, and crying and muttering incomprehensibly. I wasn't even in the zone, thank God.

The Valium I had taken had made me high, but it went unnoticed in the craziness. Tess and I got talking.

'It's hard being here with all these crazy people isn't it?'

'Yes, this is not what I meant to happen. Shall we go out for the day?'

'Oh yeh, let's. Where shall we go?'

'Dunno. What's happening in your life, besides this?'

'I need a job.'

'What do you do?'

'Office work.' Light dawns.

'I have some friends who run an agency, let's go and see them.'

'Sure, let's.'

We just put on our coats, and walk out of the place. I hadn't given Lyndsey much of a thought until then, now I wondered if she wondered whether I was OK. Anyway, too late, now I had someone else to worry about.

Tess and I took the tube, and went up to the West End. Before the days of mobile phones, how did we survive? I just marched us into Gillian's temp agency on Maddox Street and sat Tess down.

'Hey guys, Tess needs a job, can you test her skills please?'

'Elizabeth, how are you?'

Gillian and Helen knew me well. Gillian's mum and mine were old, old friends, Gillian had known me since I was 8. I didn't surprise her much, she knew my ways.

'Hello Tess, sit down.'

Half an hour later we had established that she had skills: she could type.

We had omitted to tell her where we had met, where we had come from and she never asked. We had presented a credible front and we'd got away with it. Well, Tess certainly had.

'We'll be in touch Tess, we can find you a job. What about you Elizabeth?'

'I'm fine just now, you know me.'

I smiled. Soon we would have to make our way back to the Victorian mental hospital and face the music.

They were not pleased to see us.

'Miss Green, you should take your things and leave. We will give you a bottle of pills and a paper to sign, but you should sign out.'

I was happy to do that.

'In fact, we will give you a dose now, OK?'

I leave. I don't have far to go, I'm going back to Arthur's flat, well Arthur's and my flat, in Highgate Village.

'Libby, where were you? Are you OK?'

This is Arthur's pet name for me. he sounds concerned. 'Arthur I'm OK.'

I crawl into bed. It's been a long day and sleep is welcome.

Strangely, in the morning, I can barely wake up. I try to raise my head from the pillow, what an effort. What is wrong with me?

Turns out the new medication is far stronger than before, this time I'm taking Largactil. This is a powerful drug. By 11am I am ready to stagger to college. I am not able to speak to anyone, too drugged. I feel as if I'm in a fog, people seem distant and mumbling.

After a few hours I start to leave for home.

'Wow Elizabeth, you seem so sweet and peaceful today' Jim my fellow student tells me.

Sweet, I'm dead, I'm a walking zombie. I am not present.

I DON'T QUITE MAKE
THE WALL

CHAPTER 5

May is a highly significant month in my life. Well, my old life.

I was married in May, and then, divorced in May.

Maybe I went to New York in May for the first time in many years. I'd been there before. I have pictures of me in front of the twin towers cheering on the runners for the New York marathon, balloons in hand. I was a member of World Runners, a running club running to support the end of World Hunger.

No, heaven forbid, I'm not running. I'm supporting, vital but less aggressive. Yes, we've learned how to hand out water and encourage the runners in a non-intrusive way.

For instance, I'm standing a mile from the finish line in Central Park. People are running along, some of them in their own world. It's nearly over, the last push. But you don't say that to the runners. You know, no 'Hey, only a mile to go, get on with it.'

More like 'You're doing great, looking good, nearly there.' Sometimes you can wake the runners out of their catatonia. It's as if you reached over and shook them, they look up, smile, fluff themselves up and put on a sprint towards that elusive finish line.

A few weeks later I'm watching runners in Paris. God no, still not running, I was a great supporter. My friend, as she laboured round the course, kept saying, to anyone who would listen: 'Where's the Eiffel Tower, have they moved it?'

The Eiffel Tower was the designated finish line. We laughed about that.

I had gone to New York to see my fiancé, the man I did marry, run the New York marathon. After the marathon, we did not leave together, I stayed a couple of extra days. I loved it there even then.

There was a moment after the marathon which could have come from that movie 'Sliding Doors' if you've seen it, where it showed opposite outcomes of every action.

Joe, a carpenter, a sweet man, asked me to stay in New York with him, and I was tempted by him, and by New York. I had always said: 'If only my grandfather had stayed on the boat one more stop, I'd have been American.' He left Russia in 1900 with his ten brothers and sisters to escape the pogroms. Some got off in America, he got off in England!

He was offering me the whole thing, relationship, marriage, a new life.

But I kept my word and said a reluctant goodbye to Joe, and flew back to London and got married six months later. For a long time, I wondered what would have happened if I'd stayed. In those days it was easy, less regulations and formalities.

My daughter-in-law to be is in New York for a year. It's 2009 and after a couple of visits, I have this terrific idea that I should move there.

Sort of start a new life, new identity, news friends. Won't have to find out how my family are by reading about them in the Daily Mail every day!

Hugh was my first and last Jdate in New York. After knowing him, I put myself on Black People Meet!

Hugh was old enough to know better, Annie too! Sex and sexuality were key for him, ran his life.

On my first visits to New York I stayed at Hugh's apartment, sometimes in his bed, sometimes the spare room. He kept such strange hours: up all night sleep all day. I had to amuse myself in the day and try to be helpful. Sometimes, I would make Hugh's bed, after Annie stayed over, pushing the sex toys to one side.

'Annie is the best sexual partner I ever had.'

Hugh would tell this to anyone who was listening. I thought he had a touch of Tourette's. Others did too!

At first he seemed smart and funny and intelligent. Georgia, my lovely daughter, had a coming of age trip to New York. She came on our first date.

It was a memorable day in many ways. We did the 'Sex and the City' bus tour that day and many stops later we met Hugh beside one of the lions outside the public Library in Bryant Park, poignantly, where Carrie nearly married Big in the 'Sex and the City' movie.

'I'm here.'

There's a large, not bad looking, man waving madly at us from a yellow cab stopped for a moment in the persistent traffic. God, New York is busy and crazy. My sort of city!

'Jump in.'

We jump in and the first thing he says is:

'Michael Jackson just died.'

'Oh my God.'

I realised we had witnessed the drama unfolding while we were at 'Steve's' bar, TV on in the background… A sad day!

'Do you want to have some dinner?' Hugh asks Georgia and me.

'Sure, thank you.'

This is our first meeting. He is being charming and gracious, and talking to Georgia, keeping his hands to himself. At one point he motions Georgia to move away from us for a moment, so he can whisper in my ear and arrange another meeting. Seems he's attracted … and likes me and, of course, I'm flattered. Problem of being a serial attention seeker.

So real first date, we went to the Turkish baths. I wasn't prepared. They gave me some huge knickers to wear. I could pull them up over my boobs, thank God. We got massaged, then dressed and schmoozed up on the open roof. He was a good kisser.

'You should come back and stay with me in New York.' I found out later he said that to all the women he met.

Georgia and I had stayed at the Tribeca Grand, that caring, sharing hotel, cute and boutique and not so cheap. He knew if I was to come back and see him he would have to offer me somewhere to stay.

So I started popping in and out of New York to see Hugh, who was also seeing Annie! Whilst completing buying my new house in London and moving in. Moving house and planning to move countries all at the same time was very stressful.

Then I found out that we all three were to be friends and I could go out with them on dates. So, one Saturday night we all went dancing, and then home together, to share the bed, all three of us.

But he wasn't a very caring, sharing type of guy. He wanted Annie mostly and wanted to see how we were together. I think she knew that too, so we kissed and touched a little for him. It wasn't unpleasant; other women are soft and supple, soft skin and warm, and of course, like me, less scary sometimes than men.

So he turned me over and fucked me, then her, while he pushed me to the other side of the bed, he then told me 'Elizabeth, you should go sleep in your room.'

It wasn't a nice feeling. He'd only wanted her! And for a little piece of him, I'd had to share!

He was a bully, embarrassing and bullied me in front of people. I already had one in the family. Hugh would say vulgar things.

'Elizabeth's brother is the fifth richest Jew in England,' he once announced to a room full of business people.

So I had my very own sociopath. I let him send me to a therapist, recommended by his long-time therapist. I should have ignored this expensive piece of advice. After all, not much proof his therapy had worked.

On one of my very last sessions, he insisted on coming to the session, and telling her how pitiful and weak I was. I paid her and then we went home and fucked, whilst all the time I knew this was a 'pitiful' man.

Then something good happened. His friend helped me find an apartment on the Upper West Side, near him. He insisted I live near him, controlling and bullying, he'd insisted. I found out why.

When I was away, he would let himself in with the key I had stupidly given him, and rent porn movies and watch them in my bed and jerk off!

It took me a long time to push him out of my life. He was overbearing and insistent and mean. My life was about not being included, mostly by my family, and Hugh carried that on, leaving me out on every occasion, vocally with justifications.

Being left out pushes my buttons. I always felt left out by my family and I wasn't making it up. Paranoid with good reasons? No, really good reasons! Unloved and not included were hard burdens to bear.

Before I met Hugh and started my American journey I had things to clear up in London, men to meet, places to go, and a house to buy.

One night I went on a date, a blind date set up by a girl friend.

'My friend Michael is getting divorced, and you are too. I told him about you and he's going to ask you out to dinner.'

And he did.

We went to a very fancy London restaurant, where I drank a glass of pink champagne - me, such a lightweight. I kissed him, unasked, as I went to the Ladies. I don't know if it was him, or the champagne that made me so animated.

He said what happened next was my fault because I kissed him. 'No, you let yourself be kissed,' I retorted. 'Can I drive you home?' 'Sure.'

I did not have an ulterior motive, until he said: 'Do you want to come up?'

'Yes' why not, I was thinking.

We barely made it to the living room. At 3am I woke up and said 'Do you want me to go home?'

'No.'

In the morning we made love again, took my breath away, his too.

'I feel like jello.'

He was an American.

I dropped him at Earl's Court tube station.

'Have a nice day at the office dear.'

Nothing like pretending I was the little wife.

My twice-at-night and once-in-the-morning guy became my occasional lover. He travelled so much he was hard to pin down. But I managed it.

'I don't think we should tell Rosie' he told me.

She was the one who had introduced us, introduced us for a dinner. She had no idea about what had happened, and I agreed with him, better to leave it like that. She was shocked when I told her sometime later.

But we emailed, gorgeous emails, angsty emails. I was often upset in those days, full of self-doubt and anguish. My mother didn't say anything nice, she never did. She didn't really approve of me, or my life, my style, my capabilities etc, etc.

Since I had announced my intention to divorce she was firmly on my soon-to-be-ex's side. She used to come visit us every Sunday for lunch, which involved us picking her up and taking her home, half an hour ride each way and then when she arrived she would criticize and make comments on my parenting style.

One of these Sundays I drove to Maida Vale to pick her up for lunch. Thank God David was doing the lunch. I found cooking didn't come naturally.

I ring the bell downstairs and she buzzes me in. At her door, I ring the bell.

She opens it and says:

'Oh I didn't want you to pick me up. I wanted David.'

'Fine, shall I leave you here?'

Knowing, of course, I couldn't. I drove her to my house for lunch, and I made damn sure he drove her home.

One time, Michael and I have dinner at Lemonia in Primrose Hill. It's my favourite Greek restaurant, the same waiters have been there for 35 years. I have something to tell him.

'I have a surprise for you.'

'What is it, I'm tired, you know. So much travelling.'

'I did something you suggested.'

'What was that?'

'Some waxing you suggested!'

'Really?'

I'd got his interest, in spite of his tiredness. I drove him home and we made love, twice that night as he admired my Brazilian wax.

Sometime later we emailed as he was leaving for another trip.

'I remember everything I wore on every date I went on with you,' I wrote wistfully.

'I remember everything you wore underneath.' What a sweetheart.

And then I stuck my neck out.

I'd always wanted to write. When I was 18 I told my mother I wanted to be a journalist.

'Your cousin David writes in the Daily Mail.'

'So can we invite him over and talk to him and find out what I need to do?'

'OK, I will phone him.'

But then, when he came over, they sat me down and talked to me, and told me it would be too hard for me. I was downtrodden and dissuaded. But the dream never went away.

Now, at this low time in my life I suddenly decided I wanted to write something, get some public attention, whatever spurred me on. I was also organising relationship courses at this time, taking a long look at my relationship with myself, one of the foundations of the course.

I called The Jewish Chronicle, and used my trump card.

'Hi, I'm Sir Philip Green's sister, and I would like to write a piece for the newspaper. I'm interested in relationships. I organise courses.'

I was questioned, to validate myself.

'OK, do us 1,200 words on relationships, and write about dating as well, and we need it by Friday.'

'Thank you, yes.'

It was Tuesday.

So I wrote, and my big son, a journalist, budding journalist, took off his 'son' hat and put on his 'editor' hat and sub-edited my first published piece.

I persuaded them to let me write more columns, about once a month.

But my first piece is awesome, a full page. They sent a photographer, who took a great picture, which unusually I liked. I'm happy just now, looking good. The 'getting divorced diet' worked.

I buy lots of copies of The Jewish Chronicle and keep one to put on the wall of my mother's flat.

Let me explain. her flat is the 'Philip Green shrine'. I should have run tours there, shown people his picture on every wall. People used to go there and feel bad for me.

'It looks like she's only got one child! Don't you feel bad?' I wasn't even upset that I wasn't upset.

I went to the flat with Simon, my eldest. We'd bought a frame to put my first piece on the wall. But we'd have to move something and I got cold feet.

'Let's just leave it here and we'll ask her. Scared! I was convinced she would hang it near the toilet, and I was proved right. It was hung above the toilet door, together with a beautiful picture of me and the kids. Annie her Filipino carer, practically a member of the family, had been pretty liberal with the glue and it was unreadable - specially way up there!

'Why can't it go on the wall, where it can be seen?'

'When you achieve something, I'll put you on the wall.'

Brutal, but I'm relieved. I know now I will never reach the required level of achievement. I'm off the hook. Achievement equals money in our family, one billionaire in the family is enough.

THE 89/90TH BIRTHDAY PARTY

CHAPTER 6

Michael, my beautiful and occasional lover, and I were out one night talking in a restaurant. I was so in love with this guy but kept it to myself.

'Are you in love with me?' he suddenly leaned over and asked.

'No' I said, lying.

The lie sat heavily on me and a couple of days later I told him we needed to meet.

It was a beautiful Saturday, we met in Hyde Park, it was summer, I was skinny for once. I remember in my size 10 'boyfriend' jeans!

'How are you? You look lovely' he greeted me.

How could I not love this man? There were children playing, sun shining, I was frigging nervous and jumped in.

'Sorry, my doing, I fell in love with you, and you said don't.'

I told him about what I'd learned in the relationship courses. So I owned up and took responsibility, like I'd seen people do in the courses. It was hard. Now could we be friends?

'Let me drive you home, and come in for tea, you can trust me.'

'It's not you I can't trust, it's me.'

When he called a few weeks later to say he was leaving for the US, his home, I cried, cried and thanked him for opening my heart. The course was about speaking from your heart, not your head, not as easy as it sounds.

'Don't cry, I'll cry.'

I thanked him again. We are going to be internet buddies, and he will give me dating tips, for dating on the internet, where apparently I'm going to meet the next love of my life.

I wrote him a letter, but never mailed it.

My broken heart is mending, but it's slow. If I had been a different person could I have won your unwinnable heart? Who will you give your heart to, someone I hope, even if it's not me.

The other night I realised something that I had done. I forgave myself for falling in love with you. From the moment in Wholefoods when you asked me if I was in love with you, I felt it was wrong, wrong to fall in love.

The other night I forgave myself, forgave myself for falling in love. Falling in love is OK it's what I do, women do.

Life seems to be all about not being excited. When I was a kid I think I was excited. Until Philip arrived, I was excited happy even just being the princess. Gradually the lid came down until I moved in such a small circle. Then I met you. I don't know what happened that night, it was so thrilling. Making love like that takes my breath away, takes my reason away, takes away my resolve, my reasonableness and every part of my mind that I wrestle with every day.

'Mello like jello' I think you called it. I think you were right. I remember the day I dropped you at the tube tired but happy, you were going to crawl into work and sit quietly for an hour or two til you got strong and sharp again.

I loved dropping you at the tube and wishing you a nice day at the office. Then you would text, I loved it so. Please please forgive me, I couldn't love me enough to let you love me. I couldn't trust me enough to trust your love. I couldn't find enough peace to let you find your way, choose your track, give me what you were able to give me.

Every time you texted I was so excited. I never took you for granted, pity, I should have, I should have included you like cleaning my teeth, like waking up in the morning. I just gave you hassle, like all women. You could have just been my crazy lover, my sexy American. And when you did say nice things

I was too shy to flag them up. 'You're an amazing woman' I heard you say at brunch. 'Here's your pre birthday kiss, you'll get the after birthday kiss when I get back.' 'I'm going to lay down in the bed whilst it still smells of you.'

You're just a flawed human being just like me. I need more savvy, more guile, less trust, more suspicion I want to put my guard up, keep my wits about me. Stop looking, stop searching, have peace, love myself and above all allow myself to be loved.

Looking for love is foolish, specially when you can't let it in. Feel good, look in the mirror, be slim, be gorgeous, let people love you. Let it in. I can, I let you in it must be worth the pain and heartbreak. Are you guarding your heart? Are you sad, or glad?'

And I had to go dating, because now I had to write my column, so I had to kiss frogs, date people, to have some tales to tell.

This might be beginning to look like my 'sexploits', so many men, some remembered, some not, all the sleeping around to feel loved.

I'd felt unloved forever. The sexuality started at 14, apparently it's the beginning of sexuality for girls, and I was definitely in the demographic. Aged 14 we went on what turned out to be the last family holiday with my father, to Jersey. When I was 15 he dropped dead of a heart attack on the kitchen floor whilst getting a snack. He was a compulsive eater, a trait I think I inherited.

There were gorgeous Italian waiters at the hotel in Jersey who wanted me, or at least wanted to play with me, even though I was a young 14, dressed in unsophisticated clothes by my mother, not to keep me from being a siren, but because she didn't seem all that interested, even though she herself was very chic! But just because I wasn't provocatively dressed, it didn't stop me from my sexual exploits and I played around.

One day, my father went to talk to one of the guys, to tell him to behave with his daughter. This might have been the first, and now the last, time he did a fathering duty. But the guy was in the clear, I was the one leading him on, we did everything a couple could do except … fuck! I knew this was what I wanted and it made me feel wanted, and loved. At first, I really did think it was love. Then, I knew it wasn't, it was just sex. But it was still nice, made me feel good.

Next moment I'm rationalising it in my head.

'I'm brave, it doesn't matter, it's attention and satisfying, well sometimes, and no it isn't love, but who said it is?' I thought to myself, and then, excuse the pun I just said 'fuck it' and ran around with anyone.

Some years later, all the fucking around had a consequence, which could have been serious. But it does make me smile, wryly. It was the sizzling 70's, I hadn't left for India yet. I was living in a squat.

The squat was an uninhabited house which we broke into, fixed up a little, got the electricity working and lived there. Owned by the local council, we lived rent free and the police had limited powers to move us on. I was a middle class squatter. I had a car, and nice clothes.

There were several squatters houses. We were in Finsbury Park. The nerdy people were in my squat, not the 'beautiful' people. The beautiful people lived up the street and borrowed my car, and my clothes.

Then I met Jill, friend of one of my house mates. She was how I wanted to be; wild and free, with a husband and lovers. I met one of them, Alisdair. He was so lovely we shared him.

Until one day when she came to me saying she thought she had caught something and we should visit the VD clinic.

The clinic was in Paddington, first visit for me. It didn't seem very savoury, we went in and sat on the battered chairs leaning against the white tiled walls. I suppose they didn't want to make it look too inviting. We took numbered tickets from the dispenser. This was to give us anonymity.

The loudspeaker announced 'Number 327 through the green door.'

I got up and went in. This matter was a little delicate.

'Um, my friend slept with her boyfriend on Tuesday, and I slept with him on Wednesday, and she's caught something. Do you think I could have caught something?'

The doctor did not bat an eyelid. 'OK, we'll get you tested.'

Luckily, I was clear that time. But I blamed Jill, and I told her.

While I'd been walking in the park with Michael, Tina my sister-in-law, phoned me to ask me for a list of my mother's friends, and relations, for her birthday party.

'What birthday party?'

'It's your mother's 90th birthday party, we're in the middle of organising it.'

'You know she's only 89?'

I had been expecting this call, thinking about it, making lists in my head, but for the following year.

'Yes, I know, but plans are so far along that we're doing it this year.'

'OK, I'll look up all the numbers.'

'Yes, give them to Katie please.'

Feisty Katie is my brother's PA. She needed to be that way to keep away all the people who wanted money and favours from him. I knew Katie, best to get to know everyone around who looked after my billionaire brother and his wife, best path to them!

I also realised that they had to invite me, which hadn't been the case with all his other luscious parties. This time he had no choice, people might talk and he had to be seen to be doing the right thing.

It's the night of the birthday party, October 12th, my mother's birthday, we're at the Four Seasons hotel in Hyde Park – well, not Michael, I invited him but he couldn't make it. The party was sensational.

My ex was happy that I didn't have a date. Tina had asked him if he minded me bringing someone, and he said 'Yes.'

What a bloody cheek. So I tried as hard as possible to find someone to bring. But no-one could make it. So it was just me, sitting with friends.

There was a divide in the room. My mother's table, and the family and friends tables filled one side of the room. I was not at my mother's table. Cousin Gloria and her beau Bill came from Canada to be with her, together with her best friend Phyllis and the other older ladies.

On the other side of the room were all my brother's people, the movers and shakers in business, a Lord, a couple of Knights of the realm, and the rich people. The well-dressed rich people, the people who thought they were all really something.

We were all well-dressed. Georgia and I had bought special dresses. Mine was grey tweed with a big black diamante brooch on the shoulder, Vera Wang, don't you know. Georgia wore Matthew Williamson. We looked good. Can't wear all your riches you know.

Tina wore a huge diamond, with a very low neck dress to give the diamond precedence. I have photos, it caught your eye, it glittered in the dimmed room. It was an eye catcher.

The grandchildren sat at a table all together near the back. Georgia, Jacob, Chloe and Brandon had once all been close, shared holidays on the Green family yacht, swum and played, visited exotic places. Poor Simon, my eldest, had never been included. I had pestered my mother endlessly.

'Why isn't Simon invited?'

'He's too old, how would he get on with them?'

'He would, what are you saying?'

But he wasn't invited, much to his chagrin. He knew Chloe and Brandon, but not like the other two did. he hadn't tasted the delights of jumping off a boat in the middle of the ocean, or eating at the most expensive restaurants, or shopping endlessly like Chloe and Georgia sometimes did, with no limits.

As was proven when Chloe unexpectedly joined us on a family holiday in Spain, in Philip and Tina's flat.

Georgia was with Chloe on their boat, about to leave and be flown to Spain to join us. One night near to departure, Philip was badgering Chloe to do her homework.

'If you don't do your homework, I'll make you go to Spain with Georgia.'

He had hardly finished speaking and she had her bag packed, so he had no choice. When Chloe decided something there was no fighting or reasoning with her. She had Philip, her father, round her little finger.

So they were flown on Philip's private plane, and Chloe got their driver, on her command, to stop on the way from the airport to buy them sweets. I was a tiny bit intimidated on her arrival, knowing anything I did wrong would get straight back to my disapproving brother.

I remember the first time Georgia and Jacob went on the boat with their cousins. When Georgia came home, aged 10, she seemed a little agitated.

'Mum, I've got something to tell you.'

'What, what's wrong?'

'We ate meat!'

'Is that it? Is that all?'

Turns out Georgia is now a meat and two veg girl anyway!

Chloe had a lovely time with us all in Spain, and we met the people from downstairs, the Craigs with their kids, Olly and Juliette, who became part of the gang, joined the family. They lived round the corner from us in North London, but here we met them for the first time, in Spain.

At the 89/90th birthday party, Chloe and Brandon sang grandma a song, Simon and Georgia gave a speech, and then Paul Anka sprang out on to the floor singing 'Diana', an old and treasured song. He ran among the guests, taking hugs, pictures, sharing the microphone.

I realised this was why the party went ahead, the fabulous cabaret had already been booked.

Philip made a speech, looking a tad sheepish, everyone laughed.

'Ma said to me, you've had parties, now it's my turn, I want a party for my birthday. So we started planning, and then Annie found her passport, and we discovered it was only her 89th. So happy Birthday Ma, going into your 90th year.'

She makes her grimacing smile and nods to everyone, as we clap. I'm restless, walking around, not eating, talking to people, crossing the line occasionally, to speak to Philip's friends, many of whom I know.

For the finale, Paul Anka invites my mother up on stage, and he sings a personal song to her.

I help her up, some people don't know who I am, he has no idea and just thanks me.

Then he sings a tender song, about my mother's life, details previously provided by Tina, to the tune of 'My Way', the song he wrote for Frank Sinatra:

"It's clear those near and dear

Have gathered here with admiration

We've learned

We've all discerned

You've surely earned

This celebration.

Although

Of course you know

That you are loved so in such a sure way

Alma for you

All you do

Here's my way

Your way.

God chose Ephraim and Rose

And heaven knows with love abundant

To share

A daughter rare

And raise with care in wondrous London.

Yes they kvelled

'Cause you did so well

Yes you would excel

Their sparkling diamond

16 and sweet

Soon you would meet

Your darling Simon

Each lovely home you'd well adorn

Then Philip and Elizabeth

They were born

Time with dear Simon

Wasn't long

But for your children

You were strong

With hope and pride

You would provide

And you'd raise them

Your way.

You bet

With flats to let

Your tenants get a fine safe haven

It's true Philip watched you

And now he too is a business maven

(LAUGHTER…..GIVE HIM A HAND……….WE CLAP)

Now you cruise

Roulette's your muse

And win or lose each day is like heaven

And close at hand

It's your right hand man

Your treasured Kevin

(MUCH LAUGHTER)

With friends and family you've been blessed

Because Grandma Alma

You are the best

And by your love

Their lives are fuelled

From Annie Wass

To Phyllis Gould

We wish you love

And Mazeltov

For Living

Your way."

It is so moving, I watch to see if it touches her, but hers is pretty much the only dry eye in the house. She's never been one to show any feelings, she hates the limelight, so she pretends. She gave a wry smile as I put her in her seat on the stage, a shrug and a grimace, as if to say I didn't ask for this. A couple of his lyrics make her laugh, she doesn't laugh too much either. Woman of Iron.

She loved Mrs. Thatcher, that famous 'Iron Lady'. There's a picture of them together in her flat, she admired her hugely. Someone took her to tea and stayed to hear them talk together. Seems she came across even more Iron Lady than Margaret Thatcher!

My American friend Rita was at the party. She was in London to lead a session of the 'Trusting You Are Loved' relationship course starting the next day, the wonderful course about speaking from your heart instead of your head. She sat beside me and savoured every moment.

Whenever Philip and Tina threw a party they had a professional team who made a video of the occasion. Rita got a video, everyone got a video as a memento.

When she got home she showed it to a friend who said 'Who's this Elizabeth they keep talking about? I don't see her'

Indeed, I don't see her either. She doesn't seem to have appeared much in this family.

MEETING JACKIE MASON IN MIAMI

CHAPTER 7

The dating column continued. Michael kept giving advice but there was no-one worthy of my attention. Judgmental but true.

Gloria invited me on a trip. We had not spent much time together as cousins, and she is a first cousin. Her father, Montague, known as Monty, my mother's brother, had emigrated to Canada when she was six and that's where she was brought up with her sister Pam. My mother wasn't a very family oriented person so she didn't go visit Monty, or have much contact with her nieces.

Any of her nieces; in fact I found most of them for her, some she even liked!

Gloria and Bill went to Miami for Christmas most years, because in Toronto there would be at least two feet of snow and Miami was sunshine all year round. It was winter and, yes, I would have a dose of winter sunshine please.

I had to fix up a few dates to, hopefully, find something to write about. Yes, they were Jdates, done from England though, suppose that makes Hugh not quite my first Jdate…..

I arranged three dates, and had high hopes I might meet someone on the plane. But I screwed that up by taking such an early flight. No-one handsome got up that early. Miami was a revelation. So many Jews. First time I'd felt in the majority, they were everywhere.

I bravely phone the three dates and, one by one, they cancel on me. Mind you, I'm very jet lagged so perhaps they know something I don't! I email them all to tell them about the date with the gorgeous woman they missed out on. Scott replies 'Yes, I probably did miss out.'

Man with a heart? I'm moved for a millisecond.

Gloria was older than me, we got on OK but she seemed so old in her being, and her knees hurt and she walked gingerly, and slowly. Every morning we walked along the boardwalk, in our T-shirts in the winter sunshine. I could walk twice as fast as her so I would leave her and Bill to meander while I doubled back to get a bit of speed up.

At a bar we met some people, Mitch and I struck up a conversation, and agreed to meet that night for drinks. The area was darling, the trees, palm trees, were strung with fairy lights, it looked like a fairy grotto. It was just us two. After dinner we took a stroll in the moonlight and then he invited me home, and I went.

Gloria didn't seem to mind, or disapprove or make any comments. I was a tiny bit surprised. Mitch was carrying some extra weight, Mitch was fat, flabby, out of shape. Not sexy, but a sweet guy. We had a nice breakfast on his terrace next morning, in the sunshine, but this was not going to be love, he knew and I knew. It was pleasant as we said a tender goodbye.

All my other dates had made excuses and disappeared, and I couldn't write about Mitch for The Jewish Chronicle. A one-night stand wasn't going to go down well.

I had a few more days left.

It's a beautiful, warm evening, everyone is out and walking, like us, down Lincoln Road. We sit at a table in an Italian restaurant, Gloria, Bill and I. At the next table some smart Alecs are talking about women, I introduce myself as the dating expert from England. We all start talking.

It's America, they don't mind being talked to, we have a fun conversation and I put a few myths about women straight. They're all three Jewish, the married one of course is the cutest. I have a theory about that or we can call it an 'observation'?

So seems the married men are smug and sexy … they're getting it.

The divorced men are resigned and sometimes sexy, distant memory they were once getting it.

Single men can be like rabbits in the headlights, window shopping whilst they wonder, what am I missing?

And Mitch, I just wondered whether he was dreaming about me, while I'm daydreaming about him. We women never give up the dream of finding someone special … even the not special and not sexy ones! Attention is attention.

We all say goodbye and thanks for talking and mingle with the crowds. I linger behind Bill and Gloria and a familiar face at a table catches my eye. I shake his hand and he asks: 'Do you know who I am?'

'You're Jackie Mason aren't you?'

'Yes, sit down.'

He's already eyeing me up and down.

He invites us to join him, we all sit down and I introduce Bill and Gloria. We make small talk, people stop to take photos and shake hands. He leans in close and tells me about his family, who disowned him once he gave up being a rabbi.

We take photos, and he leans in closer.

'Can I get your number?' he asks.

'Can I have lunch with you tomorrow?'

I'm slightly shocked we swap numbers. He seems keen. Is this going to be my best date in Miami? Lunch with Jackie Mason?

We speak the next day.

'Is that the English reporter?' he's nicknamed me already. 'Are we having lunch?'

I'm flattered, elated and a little scared. We arrange to meet at a kosher restaurant called Jerry's Famous Deli. It's Gloria's choice as I don't know the area.

But he's delayed as Mike, his driver, can't find the restaurant and by the time he arrives he's in a rage. But he calms down and we go to find a juice bar. He has an entourage with him, some friends from New York. My entourage is Gloria. She's my driver as well.

He sits right down beside me and asks about my family. I tell him about my famous brother.

'I hope he looks after you well,' he cracks.

'Yes.'

People can't resist talking to him as they come in and out of the juice bar, and he loves it. He plays to the gallery.

'So when are we going to have dinner? Are you busy? When can I see you?'

I get up and go to the loo.

'Let me watch you.'

I'm wearing slightly see-through cotton trousers and he watches me intently as I walk there, makes me feel uncomfortable.

When I return I ask Mike the driver: 'Is he serious?' About seeing me or anything else?

Mike nods. Oh my God, I always wanted to be famous, centre of attention, craving the attention I never got at home but being with Jackie Mason, I'm not sure I want to be that famous!

His New York friend whispers to Gloria, 'Jackie really likes her, but I think she's too young.'

Or is he too old?

I like 'too young'. Most flattering, doesn't happen too often.

He's not very cuddly and we have no physical contact but I feel his eyes on me all through lunch. We continue to laugh, he is very funny, well that's what he's known for. He has family coming to town

We speak later.

'Come and see me after dinner.' At 11pm. Now what could we be doing at that hour? I think I can guess his intentions.

I don't go. Next day he's leaving Miami. I check his number in my phone, and don't phone.

But I get my piece for The Jewish Chronicle, entitled: 'Am I Jackie Mason's date, or just part of his routine?'

LIFE WITHOUT MY FATHER

CHAPTER 8

Confession time: I eat. I eat when I'm happy, when I'm sad, when no-one loves me, when I feel neglected. I live to eat, rather than eat to live.

My father was a compulsive over-eater. He carried extra weight, as did all his family. The Green brothers were all large, is that what I inherited?

My poor father, who I barely knew, lived and worked with my mother. Think it pretty much killed him! My cousins had a theory. Allen used to say 'she killed him'. She nagged, she ruled everything. Seems she ruled him as well.

One night, in the middle of the night, my poor overweight not very healthy father came downstairs to get a snack. As he opened the cupboard to grab the Kellogg's Corn Flakes he had a heart attack and fell down dead on the floor.

Poor man, he had a different coloured pill for each day, for his weight, for his migraine, for who knows what! He had two doctors on the go who supplied him with morphine. What do you self-medicate with morphine?

He was pretty much not present. My last sad memory of him - he put me over his knee and hit me for some misdemeanor. I had been proudly wearing my new navy blouse with rows of lace all down the entire front. I had gone into the dining room to show it to him, my happiness was cut short. Smacking, not allowed these days.

So I wake up in the morning to find Uncle Harold and Auntie Claire sitting tearfully on my bed.

'What's wrong? Why are you here?'

'Your father passed away in the night.'

I struggle, passed away? What does this mean? Oh, he died, why don't they just say that?

We're Jewish, the body has to be buried fast in Jewish tradition.

The body is in the house, there is a coffin brought in and rested on chairs in our living room. Grandma Green comes over and sits and cries over the coffin. I think my father was the most decent one of the brothers, better than 'wicked Uncle Bert', or poor dead Jack or Victor who was young, much younger, and muddling his way through the world.

Ann, his sister, lived down the road with her two youngest children, Esther and Leon.

My mother rings them up. 'If you want to see your brother one last time you'd better run up the road, he's lying dead on the kitchen floor.'

Esther told me this many years later, not one to waste sentiment my mother, they ran up the road in their pyjamas.

Everything was a blur after that. My mother did not let me go to the burial ground, I should have gone. I had such a sense of incompletion that I looked for my father around every corner for the next 17 years.

My mother and I had a conversation a few days after he died which only left things further unfinished. She's sitting in the dining room when I go in tearfully.

'What will happen now?'

'Just imagine he's gone out,' she says in a bland manner 'and he won't be coming back.'

I was a young 15-year-old, young and lost. My father, in the rare interactions we had had, was on my side. Now I was left with the enemy. My brother had been sent away to boarding school so truly it was just me and my mother.

But she didn't sit around, she carried on going to business every day. She really was a businesswoman at heart. She once told me 'I wish I'd never had children, I prefer going to work.'

Not a natural mother then.

That's why my father ate. For comfort, to forget, escape. Food was calming, anaesthetising, good for anger management, and self-abuse, none of which worked. I know, I've tried them all. I think I inherited comfort eating from him, if you can inherit such a thing.

I felt lost and unloved most of my childhood. Aged three, I refused to eat, they mashed everything in the bottom of my milk. I remember I mostly ate chocolate biscuits and drank milk. I had great teeth, milk was good in those days, more nourishing. Drove my mother mad, I was already using food as a bargaining tool, as if I sensed something was wrong.

When Nelly, the Swiss nanny, came to look after us we ate healthy food, long before it was healthy. We had plain or strawberry yogurt in glass pots, delivered by the milkman with the horse and cart. Glass pots have come back again now, all these years later.

I had this privileged middle class life, or so it appeared. On Sundays we used to go ice skating at Queensway Ice rink with Vanessa Pepper, her mum and her sister. I had lessons, it was competitive and not always fun. Everything we did was to keep up with other people, or be better than them. For appearance's sake, to look good, be the best.

I went to private school, driven there every day by my parents in a multitude of different cars. My father liked cars, and changed his car often. When he bought a Bentley I was embarrassed and I wouldn't let them drop me outside the school, I made them stop round the corner. The girls at my all-girls' school were cruel. Girls were mean, nasty, pulled hair. There was scratching, name-calling and that was just when we were eight.

Bella always tells this story about my first day at school. They had all been together since they were five, I joined them three years late. I was eight when I went to my new North London school. I had 'break' with me like all the others, which I thought was for sharing, other people did too, except Bella.

'I'm not going to share anything with you,' she retorted. My first kick-back, the playground was the toughest thing about school, yes even in an all-girls' school. Survive the playground, the classroom was a doddle. Although some of the remarks on my school reports did not reflect that! Of all the things my mother could have kept from my school days, only thing she kept were my school reports. Which are funny, now!

I just stayed at the bottom of the class, I had stopped trying aged eight. I got sent out of the room unfairly, at least to me it was unfair, so I decided at that moment that rules weren't for me, and I wasn't going to try any more. I carried it out to a 'T'!

I'm in senior school now. The teachers were warned I was coming, my reputation preceded me.

Neither of us, me nor my brother, took school seriously. My brother told the headmaster of his very expensive, exclusive boys' Jewish boarding school he wanted to be a footballer, and most days he watched the man make the stained glass windows. My parents paid a lot of money for that non-compliance!

Me, I stayed bottom of the class. I acted out my anger and frustration most days, often on the piano teacher Miss Noble. I desperately needed attention and it seemed to me the only way to get it was to be naughty.

Took me such a long time to figure out you could be good, normal, gentle, kind, loving and still be noticed and praised.

But at school I didn't know this, in my nice middle-class, private girls school, where academic achievement mattered the most.

So at the bottom of the class, teachers wrote things like:

Art report, Miss Russell: Elizabeth's work is quite good but she could improve if she were more willing to listen to advice.

No change there then.

Latin (yes, Latin that 'dead' language): only fair, Elizabeth should be intelligent enough to realise the importance of thorough learning.

Or not bothering at all.

Geography: Elizabeth is responsive in class but her interest seems to be superficial.

Second from bottom. Ah well, Geography wasn't my first love, obviously.

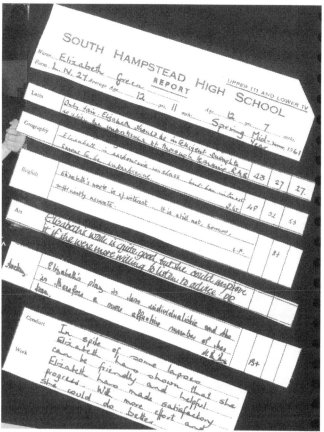

The problem wasn't intellect, it was lack of attention, feeling unloved and bored. I'd been taken to an educational psychologist aged 10 or so, who warned my mother that I had a high IQ and needed stimulation at school.

The report read:

E. MILDRED NEVILL - Educational Psychologist

Consultations—Tues., Wed., Thurs.

2 PERCEVAL AVENUE
BELSIZE LANE
HAMPSTEAD, N.W.3
Tel. SWiss Cottage 4792

Home Address. Week-end Consultations

MOORLANDS
CROYDON ROAD
REIGATE, Surrey
Tel. Reigate 2930

THIS REPORT IS PRIVATE AND CONFIDENTIAL.

Elizabeth Green was tested with the most recent revision of the Stanford-Binet Scale of Intelligence Tests on April 9th, 1959. At that time her age was 10 years and 9 months and she passed sufficient test items to give her an Intelligence Quotient of 149. This shows that she has superior mental ability of a considerably advanced order, well above the average found in schools which give the more exacting forms of education.

During the test Elizabeth was very quick to grasp requirements, although she was inclined to be hesitant when she needed to give careful explanations and she might have been a little more discerning. She has an unusually large vocabulary for her age and was most successful when dealing with other tests which have an English basis, while her ability to associate ideas was excellent. Her immediate verbal memory was accurate and she showed promise when Arithmetical Reasoning was involved.

There is no doubt that Elizabeth has a mind of decided promise, but her ability reaches too high a level not to cause certain difficulties. She is bound to be more critical and far-seeing, more ready to challenge authority and in need of plenty of outlets for her energies. She should respond well to work which contains a challenge and if once she settles down to use her powers to good advantage, she should become a credit to any school.

E. Mildred Nevill

There was a handwritten note at the bottom.

E. MILDRED NEVILL - Educational Psychologist

Consultations—Tues., Wed., Thurs.

2 PERCEVAL AVENUE
BELSIZE LANE
HAMPSTEAD, N.W.3
Tel. SWIss Cottage 4792

Home Address. Week-end Consultations

MOORLANDS
CROYDON ROAD
REIGATE, Surrey
Tel. Reigate 2930

Ap. 13 1959,

Dear Mr & Mrs Green,

Here are my reports on the children's tests which I hope you will find useful. I have sent them in duplicate so that you can have spare copies for schools.

I do hope that the trouble over Elizabeth will die down. Please let me know how she gets on next term. I shall always be interested to have news of her.

Yours sincerely
E. Mildred Nevill

But nobody took any notice. 149, 150 is genius level. I was naughty because I was bored. But they wanted to fit me back into the square hole, whilst I was determined to be a round peg. Different, always and forever!

So the days went by, every day seemed the same. My parents drove to school each morning and back late in the evening from Croydon, South London, many miles from where we lived. Nannies looked after us.

Nelly, the Swiss nanny, left and we could just eat what we liked again. Bella and I were best friends by now, and always went to the sweet shop to buy sweets on the way home from school. You could buy four fruit salads or four liquorice chews for a penny. Everyone ate sweets, no-one went to the gym. But my mother always dieted and smoked vehemently, even when she was pregnant with me. In my mind that's the reason I came out a teeny five and three-quarter pounds. Mini then, mini now! Height-wise, at least!

But I soon learned the pleasures of eating. I learned, if you loaded up on carbs, you could fall asleep, in a carb stupor, block out all the things that hurt, block out the world for a while.

Much later, I started throwing up. I wasn't a serious bulimic, I didn't rot my teeth or damage my throat. But sometimes I had to really eat a huge amount, just in order to throw up. I had many shameful rituals; favourite shops, favourite chocolate bars, secret shopping trips, just to buy 'nosh'.

Much later in life, I could phone my daughter.

'I'm in Sainsbury's buying cake, tell me to stop. Tell me to put it down and leave the shop,' and she would. That's a big ask, and a lot to admit. But I was determined my kids would not inherit my food phobias and eating foibles. Their father was slim, almost too slim, and Georgia and Jacob were a good size.

Simon, my eldest, inherited the 'Green' gene. My brother struggles with his weight and my mother, once she was in a wheelchair, just ate. She ate vanilla ice cream every day for lunch, she just let her hips spread.

I'm in her kitchen. On the side counter there are cans of Slim Fast.

'Are you still dieting?'

'Mind your own business. I can do what I want.'

Sometimes, round at her flat on arrival I would ask her politely:

'How are you today?'

'Why are you asking?' she would say brusquely, alternatively she would reply tersely and say 'Surviving.'

She never cut me any slack. I was always wrong, seemingly a disappointment, not a big achiever, and never slim enough.

One day, walking in Willesden, North London, I found a self-improvement centre and started taking their courses. A few of the people wore orange clothes, with a mala of beads round their necks, celebrating their guru in India.

I felt a strong pull to go inside, get away from my life here in London. Run away, as fast as possible. I had worked for a little, teaching, my second choice after journalism. But I didn't really want to be a teacher so it's funny I call it a 'choice'. I was pretty much left to my own devices, no-one cared what I was going to do, the attention was all on the prince!

As my teaching practice began at Loughton College in Essex, I was excited.

I don't remember anything about it, except Donald, my head of department.

My first day there, I was wearing a cute short-sleeve brown and white smock, to hide a few extra pounds, and we were attracted instantly. He looked at me, that look men give you when something stirs! I remember that. I remember meeting his other half, Christine, who also taught there, so I was a little wary, but that seemed to make me more enticing, damn it.

Princess Anne, the Queen's daughter, was getting married, and the whole country had a public holiday to celebrate. Donald and I celebrated in my bed at the squat. We raised a glass at the appointed moment.

Yes, seems I just rolled from bed to bed. It was easier with Donald, I knew this could never be put on a permanent footing, so there was nothing to lose except perhaps a little dignity on my part, and I don't think I had much dignity in those days. I did not like myself, I was not worthy, as I kept proving time and time again.

I mean, it wasn't anything I did, was it? Did I flirt? Did I portray my wanton side? What was I inviting? Did I keep inviting?

I told myself I wanted to be married, be in a solid relationship, or did I? Did I just want sex and drugs and rock and roll? Actually, I wanted much more than that. I wanted all the love I never had, all wrapped up with a bow. I wanted someone to love me to the moon and back, take me in their arms and keep me safe.

I still joke now when I meet someone nice 'could you just take me in your arms, and hug me for a week?' Thinking, that will do for a start.

Actually, I'm much stronger than that, I know I have to love myself, in order to be loveable. Have to think I'm good enough, special enough, clever enough, smart and funny with great self-esteem. My childhood did not provide me with much of that, and I've worked damn hard to achieve those qualities and feelings now.

I have the most active mind, which derails me at every turn. If I phone you, and you don't pick the phone up, I know it's because you don't like me, you're avoiding me, or if it's a man I'm not good enough for you, for sure.

Of course it may just be you're out, busy, at the movies or in a meeting!

I have the most vivid imagination. Intellectually, I know what's going on; emotionally, I'm a quivering 10-year-old, most unattractive and unappealing.

But at least I recognise that part, and see it reaching up and grabbing me. I can apologise for it, explain it, explain it away and watch for my warm, loving self to return, which it always does.

When I got to India, even the guru told me: 'If you want to die I will give you a better way than eating yourself to death.'

JOHN KELLY BOYS SCHOOL

CHAPTER 9

Being Jewish is like belonging to a huge, global family who are all united, same customs, same rituals, and I don't just mean the chicken soup!

I mean the shouting, that's how many of us Jewish families communicate. Mine did!

In my family the shouting never ended. My mother confided in me once that she thought criticism was a form of communication. In that case, she was a good communicator.

I married my mother. My mother and David both gave me the same treatment, they were ardent fans of each other. Silently, and sometimes not so silently, he applauded the way she treated me, spoke to me, was scathing with me, and criticised me. Then followed up with his own version.

I was shy as a child, shy and seems I knew something was not right from the beginning as I resisted eating my food. I had a wicked mind of my own, it exasperated my mother.

I was born in Croydon, Surrey. It was more like country then, now it's nearly part of South London it seems. We lived in a flat above my father's television and radio shop, Thoroughgood Radio, Tamworth Road.

When Philip met Kate Moss many, many years later, the story goes, she said 'You're a boy from South London and I'm a girl from South London, let's do business.'

Cute, even if it's not true, and they did.

Tamworth Road became famous, one night in 1952, as a big crime story unfolded directly across the road. Bentley and Craig, aged 19 and 16, were on the roof of the warehouse opposite with a gun and shot a policeman. Bentley screamed out the infamous words 'Let him have it Chris'.

Did he mean give the policeman the gun? Or let him have it - the bullet?

Poor mentally challenged Derek Bentley was hanged for the shooting, although it was actually Christopher Craig who fired the fatal shot.

Craig, however, was too young to hang.

Many, many years later, Bentley was given a posthumous pardon.

Guns and shootings in those days were so rare in sleepy Croydon in Surrey. Still are.

We lived there until I was eight, then we moved to North London, the 'Jewish' area, Hampstead Garden Suburb. Gillian, my friend to this day, tells me I was so shy I hardly spoke to anyone when she came to visit with her family. Standing against the wall, seems I wanted to shrink into it. Afraid of my own shadow I have carried that with me. Fight it most days.

What is the fear? Of not being loved, not being loveable? I'm a tender, sensitive Cancerian, tough on the outside, heart of gold on the inside. Cancer, sign of the moon, on full moon sometimes my reason wavers, deserts me, it gets black for a moment, doubts flood in.

My kids shout at me too, specially my eldest son. He saw so many stormy, unpleasant encounters between me and my mother, and my brother. I think he made it OK to speak that way.

One Christmas he tried to stand up for me, at the Green family Christmas dinner at China Tang in the Dorchester, Park Lane.

Yes, for two years in a row the Green family had a Christmas dinner and we were invited. Two years was enough, after all what gifts do you buy for the people who have everything?

Georgia and I had our version of a Buddhist koan. It's a riddle to help them to enlightenment. 'If you're Tina Green, is it still fun going shopping?'

Picture this: we're sitting round a huge table, the Filipino maids are sitting at their own table in the corner. We start handing out gifts, I'm a little excited as know I will get a gift, just one, hopefully something expensive. The others are in a frenzy of divinely wrapped presents each more exotic than the last.

Our one package is small and my kids rip open the paper. Jacob is sitting with Brandon, Philip's son, similar ages, know each other well. Simon is further round the table sitting with his grandmother, I am sitting with Georgia. Tina is near us. She's started in on the wine already, does she know something we don't?

I have a gift for Philip, the billionaire. I have a book signed by the author, a comedian who came and spoke at the boy's school. I have no idea if Philip's ever heard of him, or has the time or inclination to read, ever. But it seems thoughtful and appropriate, so I thought.

The kids have iPods, oh my God, just what I wanted. I open my small package, and out falls a tiny Gucci bag, almost doll size. Now I have to look happy and excited, and I wanted an iPod.

Philip, meanwhile, has opened my gift, somewhere in the melee is a card full of thank yous, and thank yous, he is generous, and likes to be thanked, at least I know that part.

Suddenly he starts screaming at me, in front of family and friends.

'Is this what you buy me? A book? After everything I do for you? Why didn't you get me a tie? Something useful.'

He's really screaming.

'Even a tie from Marks and Spencer would have done, any tie.'

I don't know which way to turn and everybody freezes. Tina just keeps sipping.

Simon stands up and says to him, and the whole room 'Don't shout at my mum, she didn't do anything wrong. Leave her alone.'

My mother grabs him. 'Sit down, don't interfere, stop.'

Philip is about to turn on him, so he sits down abruptly.

Jacob tells me later Brandon turned to him and said 'Keep your head down, we're in the eye of the storm.'

'Where's the card, I wrote you a great card?'

But it's too late and I'm crushed. Chloe and Brandon have opened the gifts I got them, with no comment. Better at least than being screamed at.

Thank God, it's near the end of the evening and they are leaving soon for Northolt to catch their private plane to Sandy Lane in Barbados. Where Father Christmas will ride up to the beach on a jet ski, and the weather and the food are expensive and exquisite.

I think Tina is now past caring, she goes round the table, says her goodbyes and hugs everyone, even I get a conciliatory hug.

Chloe comes up to me and says, 'My dad's an idiot, I'm sorry.' They leave for Barbados and I leave for peace and quiet.

But I don't stand a hope in hell. My kids have seen it all, licence to yell and abuse.

So here I am aged eight and … Jewish, who knew?

Aged three, I had a taste of being Jewish. I was a bridesmaid for wicked Uncle Bert, my father's eldest brother, and got a 'Mogen Dovid' star of David on a chain. But something was wrong with mine, so they took it away to get fixed and I'm still waiting for its return.

My first day at new school, South Hampstead High School, and aged eight I'm waiting nervously as the new girl to meet the girls. My mother says 'If they ask you if you want Jewish prayers or non-Jewish prayers, say Jewish.'

OK, got an identity at last, but what the hell is she talking about?

So I went to Jewish prayers. But worse was to come. Hebrew classes, every Sunday morning, I was eight in the class with the five year olds. Thank God I was small, small but perfectly formed. Pretty, and pretty fearful.

People terrified me.

That's the dilemma.

I have huge expectations. I'm lying in bed looking at it. Is it wrong to want everything? To wake up and want to be loved, to want to wake up next to someone, to want to matter and many other things.

So what would it be like to walk fearless through the world?

To never be shouted at nor demeaned!

To never mind not being invited.

To have a warm and loving family. That makes me scared and faint.

To feel so sure of myself that I never obsess again about any man, or relationship.

To never again need to beg for love.

To love myself and want to diet.

To be loved with condition …

To be loved beyond condition …

To speak, and be heard.

To have a job, be part of the group. Not always have to be the leader. To get up every morning fit for purpose.

To not have everything I do put down and reviled.

To cry and know I can stop.

To be a size 6 … American

To be an American

To belong … somewhere

To be adored

To wake up in loving arms every morning

To look forwards not backwards

To think everything's possible, because it is

To not hear criticism in everything.

To never take things personally ever again.

To be rich in spirit, heart, and soul.

To keep loving and wear my heart on my sleeve!

To never give up

To never, never, never give up

To sleep and have sweet dreams

Next to the man of my dreams

To remember things.

To remember what I went upstairs for

To remember I am loved

And to write something wonderful that the world will see

And not to care what people think

To stand tall and stride like a giant through the world.

The best things come in small packages.

To drive in New York.

In a Zip car!

To marry for love.

I don't mind about a Ketubah now

Nor smashing the glass

I will shout Mazeltov in my heart

I will not allow myself to be screamed at any more

By the billionaire, nor his wife, nor his children, nor his forebears, nor my forefathers. Nor anyone.....

I will have it tattooed on my arse, 'thank you Philip, thank you for looking after me, for paying for me, for bankrolling me, for giving me money......and giving me grief, much grief.'

Actually it will be MUCH less than that, I'm planning to have a much smaller arse, sometime soon.

I will dream, I will daydream

I will find love

Wait, love will find me

But I will find heaven along the way

I will still love all my loves

And hold a candle for you all, a candle of hope and prayer that you start to love, as only I know you can

Let everyone in, all of you, the way you've let me in

Rejoice

Be happy

I'm going to be from now on

I'm not going to rush to call people any more

I'm going to sit back, and be an opening, to be called…..
everyday…..by someone special

I'm going to start saying NO, NO, NO

NO will be my new YES

I will remind myself as I walk round Central Park

Everyday

In New York

A poem written in the style [I hope] of the Liverpool poets in the 60s:

RELIGION

Don't marry out
It's nothing to shout about
You won't create community
Nor opportunity
You'll be sorry
Your parents will worry

He won't know chicken soup
You'll be out of the loop
Matzo balls – what's that?
Wearing a hat
Ridiculous don't worry
It'll suit you when you get fat

Mind you I didn't meet the kids at Jewish playgroup
Nor go to Israel when I was a teen
Sometimes I wonder – where had I been
When you were all mingling and mixing
And meeting your future brides aged 5

I lived in a family where I didn't know I was Jewish
In fact til they told me aged 8
The idea was quite newish
You're Jewish!

I LOVE YOU,
I'M SORRY,
PLEASE FORGIVE ME,
THANK YOU

CHAPTER 10

LETTER FROM MAHESH 14th September 1980

Hi? Beautiful – it was really nice reading your letter – as days go by I get more and more certain that my life is imitating a B grade Hindi movie – full of twists and turns – melodrama – and all that stuff a movie is made of – now look at the way you got to hear about me- there I was going for my shooting when Miss Green suddenly springs up and talks, talks (your letter) of sweet nothings. Damn it you should have at least written a few abuses to me – after all that was no way to treat a lady – the last time we parted ways.

Anyway you have only confirmed again what I always thought of you, you are a sweetheart. I gave up Rajneesh about 2 and a half years ago. Yes, I have heard of EST my friend Shabana (film star female) did one group. I have no idea whats it all about I have gone through a lot in the last 2 and a half years. Yes, Parveen went off her head – one year ago she had a mental breakdown – yeah! Insane she took about 9 months to get back to normal – but once you have a crack-up you are never the same. Those were the most trying days of my life – I am no longer living with her – I know I can be of greater help to her from a distance.

Miss Green I really went through excruciating pain over the last few years – but - even suffering ends. I did come to London twice last year I was there for about 15 days. I would love to come (soon) again – yeah will you mother me – take care of me – fuss over me- fuck me- bathe me- feed me- come to the movies with me?

Let me know your phone no – I could talk to you – Bombay-London is now direct dial.

That's all sweet heart nothing profound to say – yeah! I do feel great affection for the girl Veena as the images of the past flash through my head –

Thanks for everything. Write again. Lots of love etc.

Mahesh

JULY 11th, 1976
VEENA IS BORN

CHAPTER 11

What am I doing here? How did I get here to the subcontinent? I had not been happy in damp England for a long time.

I'm in North West London, on a leafy street walking past a large rambling Victorian house. A large sign outside says 'Quaesitor'. I found out later it means 'searcher'.

'EVERYONE WELCOME, COURSES, MEDITATIONS, MASSAGE.'

Every hippie hackle on my body responded and I went inside.

This was the first time I saw all these people wearing orange, a colour I learned to love and then hate, and then not wear for 20 years.

It's in vogue again now.

They had wooden beads round their necks, the 'orange' people, long strings down to their navels with a small plastic-coated disc enshrining a picture of the guru 'Bhagwan Rajneesh', a kindly looking, twinkling old man with a long, grey tinged beard, and I found out later, a great line in hats. The string of beads is called a mala.

People spoke lovingly of the master and told me they were all planning to go see him in Poona, in India. First time India came into my consciousness. I wasn't picturing myself as a 'sannyasin' as the disciples were known. Not at this point!

I made other wonderful discoveries at Quaesitor. I discovered a meditation group, and I got a therapist, a South African named Simon, my father's name, how apt.

Best session I ever had with him - hands down - happened one evening, as I rushed in exhausted after work.

'I'm so tired, I just want to lie down and sleep.'

'You should,' he said and that's what I did while he watched over me.

Sometime later I awoke refreshed.

'That's the end of the session,' he told me.

I was a little puzzled, bewildered, full of sleep. So I just nodded dumbly.

Good value, or waste of money? He made me pay, jury's still out.

Simon had a gathering one day and asked us all to bring our favourite music. Someone brought Bob Marley. I loved him then, and ever since.

I did not know, but I was now on the road to India – as I valiantly tackled my first teaching job. The one my mother disapproved of because it wasn't a 'nice' school.

Now I met Poonam – high priestess. Her husband, Teertha, lived in the inner sanctum in Poona. Vivek was Bhagwan's right-hand woman, Teertha was his right-hand man. I wasn't much involved in the inner workings of the ashram, just the inner workings of myself, soul searching, looking for love. I found out Bhagwan would take care of all that. My job was to surrender, and I tried hard!

I did some meditations with Poonam, enlightenment intensives – I was pretty much the only one not in orange. You sat facing each other on the floor. Taking turns, long turns – we would start with the question 'who am I?' Asking and asking. The listener just sat and looked – first in one eye, then in the other. Then past my eyes, then back. Sometimes, I would hold their gaze – sometimes not!

Extraordinarily, the answer would start to bubble up and become clear. I don't remember the answer – maybe it wasn't words. I would repeat the question, again and again, until it popped. It just sort of landed on me. You could see it reflected in their eyes, shining, mine too, I could feel it in my body.

Would enlightenment look like this? Shiny?

Then Poonam asked me if I would take Soma, her daughter, to India to see her father, Teertha.

I was, at this time, trying to be a teacher, not my first choice in career, so the many distractions were welcome.

'Yes, I'd love to.'

So that's what happened.

I'm getting ready to go to Poona, to meet the guru. I'm taking Soma, aged 10, to meet her dad, Teertha, one of the senior disciples. All I have to do is get her there and hand her over.

Meanwhile, I spend time with her and her sister, Rani. Just to get to know her as we're going to be on a long, long flight together. I like kids, these are great kids, with unusual parents. Soma is obviously not her birth name, I will also get a new name when I arrive.

My experience of small girls was somewhat limited, as was my experience of long-haul plane trips, and now here I was combining the two.

Soma and I are at the airport. She's very distraught, and screaming loudly, as I pull her by the hand through the airport.

No one seems bothered, so if I was kidnapping her I would have got away with it. It was before the days of heavy security, where you can't even take a bottle of water through. In those days you could pull screaming 10-year-olds through with no impediment.

We made it to the plane and threw ourselves gratefully into our economy seats for the long trip.

A stewardess passed by.

'How are you ma'am?'

'I'm ok, how long is the trip to Bombay?'

'Bombay?' she said sounding a little puzzled 'I'm not sure we're stopping in Bombay.'

'WHAT? Please could you go and check?' I'd got Soma this far, more would be stretching it.

A minute or two later she reappeared.

'So sorry, first stop Bombay, nine and a half hours.'

Soma became a little more settled, now she's on the way to see her father and she's becoming happier minute by minute.

It's a long flight, including the nearly five-hour time difference, and then we step into the heat.

A driver is there to meet us with bottles of cooled water. He tells us: 'It will be cooler in Poona.'

Poona was nice and temperate. The British Raj took their ladies there in the summer to escape the heat, and as we drove along the dusty roads, it was very green, could almost have been the Welsh countryside in parts. Except in Wales there are no buffalos in the streets and people squatting to do their toilet in the ditches.

Eventually, we arrive at the ashram. We bounce along an unmade road: this is Koregon Park, home to the ashram. We stop outside a distinguished looking house, curious and new and very far away from anything I know.

A tall bearded man comes out and Soma runs into his arms and is gone, and suddenly I'm alone in Poona, India.

They arranged a place for me to live for my six week sojourn now we drive there and I meet my cute Australian flatmate and sink gratefully on to a thin mattress on the stone floor.

'I'm tired, thank you.'

'You better sleep, tomorrow is Guru Purnima day, when everyone comes to celebrate their guru. There will be lots of people, many, many Indians. Do you have something orange to wear?'

I don't remember anything else and then it's morning and I'm dashing to the ashram in my one orange dress in a rickshaw with Anand.

He deposits me there and is gone.

I'm taken to Darshan. It's a meeting with the master, Bhagwan Rajneesh. I will sit at his feet and receive a new name and wear a mala, just like the people in leafy North London.

There's a whole procession of us, from many nations, all receiving new names. It's an overwhelming moment. I steal a glance into his eyes, it's like falling into warm pools of water. In later days there will be a chance to speak, but right now there are no words as I move into this new world.

He addresses me.

'You will be Ma Deva Veena, divine musical instrument of the master, you will serve me well.'

There is one other woman called Veena, different prefix, she's tall and South African. Subsequently, we meet.

I wonder to myself: is this what love feels like? Was that love in his eyes, love and care - the big things missing in my life. People had told me it would feel like this, so far they'd been right.

Next morning all the fervent Indians have left and things are back to normal, except this is all still far from normal. We're lining up in the morning dew, in silence to enter Lao Tzu Auditorium. The loudest noise is the birds singing, my orange shawl is a necessity. Anand is for once close by, and points out some people.

It's winter and other people have left England and the cold to look for enlightenment.

Rajneesh enters wearing one of his many hats, flanked by orange-clad disciples. Teertha, Soma's father, is there, the only one I know and others I will get to know. Although we're sitting on a hard stone floor his voice is soothing and soon I'm dozing off, travelling and jet lag got me. Bhagwan says you can get his message even asleep.

Outside, the day starts to shape up to its usual hustle and bustle.

'Will you come to Greenfields with us?' A beautiful blonde Swedish woman was inviting me.

'What is Greenfields? I mean, yes, I'd love to.'

We walk to the made-up road at the end of Koregan Park and she tells me she's Gandha. The Indians watch us walk along Koregan Park. We are the decadent Westerners, we show affection in public, kiss, even smoke workmen's cigarettes, beedies, and we're wearing their 'holy' colour. Traditionally, poor holy men became sannyasins. Now we are sannyasins, wearing orange, and acting out in public.

The Indians are fascinated and horrified, they whistle and cat call. Even in movies there was no kissing, and certainly no sex. Two raindrops would run down a window, merging, like the merging of two bodies in a sexual act. That was it!

Gandha and I take a rickshaw down Mahatma Gandhi road, the main street, to the most western looking café on the street. Here, I discover delicious slightly set curd, served in small glass dishes, served by elderly Indian men in white jackets.

An arty looking woman joins us, this is my new best friend to be, Vasudha. She's Italian and, temperament wise, nearest to me. I become an honorary Italian as the days go by!

Greenfields will become one of my eating refuge places, they have sweet little cakes, and other Indian sweets, because of course eating is the Indian national pastime and it is near the mango pulp stand, another treat not to be ignored. I was warned, people looked on India with disdain as I discovered when I told people I would be going there:

'Be careful, it's so dirty, and poor, and they don't eat meat. You will catch something. Be careful where you buy food from, make sure it's clean.'

So, that certainly didn't include the mango pulp stand on the street, where I frequently stopped for Alphonso mango pulped with cream on top, and never got sick until I'd been in India two years.

'I'm Veena,' I say to Vasudha.

'What work will you be doing in the ashram?'

'I didn't know I had to work?'

'Everybody works at the ashram, you could be cleaning toilets, be careful. Or making enlightenment food in the café with Deeksha.'

'Where do I go to find out?'

'You go to see Ma Sheela in the office, I'm going there I will take you there now.'

'Thanks. Where do you live?'

'I'm at the River House with Shanti, you must come and see us.'

'Love to' and I go, often.

Back at the ashram I go to the office and, sure enough, I am given a cleaning job.

'Damn, I don't do cleaning at home in England.'

'Yes, but it's not cleaning they're interested in here, treat it like a meditation, look inside while you're doing it, it's something to do while you're cleaning your inside.'

Thank you, Vasudha, sounds very wise.

But looking inside is the thing that scares me most. I left England to get away from my mother, from whom I had awaited praise, any faint praise, for a long time, before realising it wasn't coming. Now I'm among strangers, fabulous in a way, because I get to start again, they don't know me. Hoping I left my lack of self-confidence and low self-worth behind me in England, I'm now ready to look for love with a wonderful man.

I'd been told I could go to see Bhagwan again soon, another name for Rajneesh. I had many questions burning inside; some smart, some probably not so smart!

So making the most of the rest of the day, before I start cleaning, I wander round and check out the men! The Indian men are quite cute too, hope they like us Westerners.

Back to my sparse apartment at the Guru Prasad building, to get ready for … cleaning!

MEDITATION AND MEN

CHAPTER 12

After a few weeks I had a routine. I moved to Sunder Lodge, built on stilts, my new neighbours were Paritosh and Pradeepa, so much more exotic than Chris and Sue, their English names.

I had so few possessions and it was easy to get by, here among the trees in a new foreign land.

Vasudha and I visited the tailor in Mahatma Gandhi Road to embellish my new orange wardrobe. We have chosen the fabric, the tailor, a little gnarled old man starts pinning.

As an off-the-shelf girl I have no idea where the darts should go.

'Hey, Vasudha, help me - where should the darts go?'

Thank God she's a seamstress, creating beautiful garments to ship back to her native Italy, using some of the delicious fabrics of India. Silk is India's gold, there were places to go to buy beautiful barely worn saris to make into clothes for export.

'Hey, stand still' she chides, 'He'll put the pins in you.'

So entrenched into my new life, I'm rushing her so we can get back for Nataraj, the afternoon meditation. I'd done it in London at the Bell Street Centre, a small, dark basement. Here, it seems enchanted as we dance in the auditorium, open on all sides with the sun streaming in. Here, we can search freedom, freedom of the soul, Rajneesh's gift.

The meditation is 45 minutes of dancing, then 15 minutes of stillness while you watch the stillness, your breath, your surroundings. I have learned to stand like a statue just watching the rise and fall of my breathing. Is this all there is to do to achieve peace of mind? Who knew?

It's amazing how varied 15 minutes can be, an eternity and sometimes but a mere moment. After the final gong, I start looking around to find Suraj.

Suraj is a beautiful blond Englishman. He's standing on the edge of the auditorium.

'I'm so glad you're here, hug me.'

We hug.

'Let's have tea.'

The men have started to notice me. That's not the problem, the problem is keeping one. Is this a keeper?

The café in the ashram is run by Deeksha, a large and volatile Italian woman. If you worked in the café for Deeksha, creating enlightenment food and you made a mistake, you would hear her voice all over the ashram chiding you. In fact, more than chiding: screaming and shouting and insulting you. Apparently, this is part of healing, becoming whole, and working in the kitchen producing food is the thing to do whilst looking inside and healing!

The food there is pretty good, and we eat and drink, not too much before our dinner outing!

Tonight, we're going to have dinner at the River House with Shanti and Vasudha. I'm wondering what this Welshman could be like to have tamed this feisty, wonderful, creative Italian woman. I don't have a bicycle, the standard form of transport in Poona. Why not? I would probably need a child-sized bike and have decided to spare myself the embarrassment and difficulty of riding one.

Rickshaws for me, and Vasudha too, we're going to be ladies together.

'Don't come too late,' Vasudha had told us 'I want to show you the river.'

'How gorgeous, do you have a boat?'

'Yes, we shall float on the river for a while before the pasta.' Oh an Italian hostess, Italian food, yum. This international community sure gives you the best of everything.

'What are these black fruit on the trees?' I ask as we float beneath them.

'Those aren't fruits, they're bats' Shanti informs us.

'Oh no.' I can't help shuddering. When I've stopped shaking I take a closer look. They are delicate little creatures spreading their web-like wings, and making a strange noise. 'How horrible.'

After supper, Vasudha shows us the garments she has designed and is hoping to produce here in India and then ship to Italy. Many of the sannyasins had little businesses on the side, as a form of income shipping wonderful Indian goods, fabrics, clothing they have designed to the grateful westerners. Everything gets a good price, even beedies, the workman's cigarette. In London, middle class hippies smoke them.

Suraj and I took a rickshaw back to Sunder Lodge where he spent the night. I looked at him in the dark, and I can feel my heart melting.

'Am I falling in love?' Damn, I fall in love with everyone. If they show me a little love and care, I'm theirs, terrible habit. But I so want to be loved. It's like an ache inside. Bhagwan told us in lecture: 'A life without love is not a life worth living.'

Oh how I know that, the same way I know how my hunger drives men away, my need and greed is too much for most. But here with the master I have the determination to find someone. I love and despise myself in almost equal measure, everyone is too good, and not good enough. My mother once told me that. It is hard to shake off.

Bhagwan told us constantly to surrender.

I pondered in the dark.

'That must be why you have us surrender to you, so in life we can surrender in love, to a man, a human master. Surrendering is very powerful, it's not just giving into the man and giving the power away. It's so much more hard to discover, it's a letting go, finding peace and acceptance, letting love come in, being in charge of oneself and one's feelings. Part of me knows that it doesn't matter who, which man, and yet my ego wants to choose.'

It's not been long I've meditated in the ashram, and yet it seems Rajneesh talks much on love and surrender, and now in the dark I'm wrestling with it, much as I wrestled with Suraj's naked body when we made love.

'Will it be you Suraj? Will I fall in love with you?'

I'm sighing as I try to sleep, impossible with such an active mind, and I have to get up early to clean the bathrooms before meditating.

Why does everything seem so hard and unreachable?

MY INDIAN SWEETIE

CHAPTER 13

It's evening time, the light is beautiful in Poona as the sun sets, and we're all standing in shimmering orange robes at the gates of Lao Tzu House, waiting to go into Bhagwan's inner sanctum and have Darshan with the master.

It's a special moment to sit at the feet of the master, have him shine his light on you, be given the chance to ask him a question, in my case, probably a foolish question. It's a privilege, he treats every question as special and meaningful even when he teases. That's my feeling of foolishness about my question.

Vasudha is at the gate.

'Vasudha, I sat right at his feet, so scary at first, then I looked, it was like falling in love.'

She looked at my shining face and hugged me.

Gandha was also at the gate. We made such a contrasting couple - she tall and blonde, me petite and a little plump. We're watching who goes in and out. Two Indians wearing orange came out almost our mirror image, one tall and handsome, one shorter and plumper with a not unpleasant face.

'Girls,' the handsome one said. 'Are you waiting for someone? I'm Vinod and this is my friend Mahesh.'

God, was he handsome, and smouldering and his eye was on Gandha, I stood back to let the beautiful people take each other in.

'Shall we go for a drink at the Blue Diamond?' At the end of the unmade road of Koregan Park is the local 5-star hotel. Mind you, 5 stars in this part of India is probably not the same as 5 stars in a big city, but fancy nevertheless, and Vinod and Mahesh are staying there.

Gandha, I'm wishing under my breath, do not say no. My future hangs in her hands.

'I'd love to, with my friend.' She's gesturing in my direction.

'Of course, delighted.'

We start walking down the road, Vinod holds Gandha's slim arm so she won't slip. We walk at a respectful distance behind them. Mahesh is a sweetie, I'm enjoying this.

Of course, at this point we have no idea who we've snagged, and usually, the Blue Diamond does not like sannyasins, even sannyasins with money. But, with these Indians beside us, everyone is backing up out of the way, even staring a little.

'OK, what's going on Mahesh?'

'Vinod is one of India's leading movie stars.'

'And you?'

'I'm just a film director.'

After a couple of drinks, the love-struck couple move towards the bedroom. We're watching and giggling, mine is a lovely man I'm discovering.

'We're all in one room, are you coming with me?'

'I am,' as I'm saying to myself I should keep an eye on Gandha, who has got swept up in Vinod's charms.

It was a strange night. We listened while they made love, seems they forgot about us. Me and Mahesh, we caressed and kissed, my cute, tubby Indian.

In the morning we left them alone, so we could also have some alone time. 'Let's take a rickshaw and ride out into the countryside, and spend a little together time.'

'Wonderful.'

This man is kind of special I'm thinking, I'm rather entranced, although it started in such impersonal circumstances, an adjunct to Vinod and Gandha. Their caretakers!

We snuggle in the rickshaw!

'If I were to put you in my films there would be leaves falling. They would be playing Lara's theme, we would run towards each other arms outstretched.' He stretched out his arms to me as he spoke, I loved it, I was completely drawn in. God, this man was irresistible.

'I have to go back, jobs to do. How often do you come to Poona?'

'Once a month. Will you wait for me my little fatty bum bum?'

He was so cheeky and enticing, from him these words were sweet. I am in heaven.

'We'd better get back.'

I nodded. I was dying to tell everyone about my catch. In my mind I'm already in my first major movie, in the starring role. After all, hadn't Bhagwan told me that I had the right build to be an Indian movie star, and now he had provided the director, and not just any director, but the enfant terrible, the bad boy who throws chairs at censors, makes immoral films and is blacklisted. How delicious.

He brought me back to the ashram gates where we found Vinod waiting by his limousine with Gandha. We wave them goodbye and as soon as the car was out of sight round the corner, we jumped on each other. We hugged, and punched the air, both drunk on love.

'Oh my God Veena, he's wonderful. How was yours?'

'Cute, funny, cuddly … and not here for a month.'

'Vinod is a huge movie star, and I've never seen any of his films, I know nothing about him. I have a wild idea. Will you come across town with me this afternoon and see a movie of his. I know we won't understand a word, but he told me he's always the villain. There are train crashes, births, deaths, marriages and he always gets the girl. Will you come?'

'God, sounds just my sort of film. No seriously, of course I will. I've never been further than Mahatma Gandhi Road and sometimes it seems so hemmed in, so here's to adventure. I'll meet you here at 2pm.'

I meet my co-conspirator, Gandha, at 2pm in front of the ashram, and we jump into a rickshaw and drive across town, through slums and shanties, men and women squatting in the streets, to a sleazy looking cinema.

I know that movies in India are like the life-blood of the people. Poor people, rich people, any people lived and died for their heroes and villains. The cinemas were full to bursting point with mostly lower caste men with grubby lungis and dhotis tied around them. The women were probably on the building site. We'd seen this as we drove all the way across town, the women were carrying bricks and rubble on their heads in small trays balanced carefully. They were wearing saris and had to hold them up to negotiate the rough terrain. We had wondered at the time, where were the men? Now we knew.

The lights went down. Vinod looked even more handsome in the film. The film was just a swirl of dancing and singing, pain and pathos. The audience cheered and shouted, it was full audience participation. Nothing like going to a movie in London.

We rushed back to the ashram, back to the familiar white faces. I mixed with Indians, why come all the way to India just to mix with a bunch of Westerners? Sidarji, the large turbaned Sikh, was on the gate. We greeted each other warmly.

Now of course I had a real Indian boyfriend, Mahesh.

No need for Suraj to know, nor any of the others I have my eye on. How delicious, I thought to myself with a sigh. Gandha was smitten as well.

Now we had to sit out the month. One whole long month.

KITCHEN MEDITATION WITH DEEKSHA

CHAPTER 14

I'm a yearner. If you show me love, I'm yours, usually forever. I will ache and burn in all the right places. I want your body, your mind, your soul. Now.

Thank goodness Mahesh was away for a month, unreachable, uncontactable. I ate slept and dreamed Mahesh, but he never knew. No time or inclination for Suraj!

Meanwhile, I made some new friends. There were Italians, other Italians besides Vasudha and they treated me as an honourary Italian. I took that as a compliment, referring to my fiery temper no doubt, the problem that had so hounded me in London. I met the beautiful Texans, Bodhiesatva, Madhuri, Deepesh and Leena. How we laughed at the thought of Bodhie walking down the street in Dallas in an orange robe. There you had to be a tough guy! Perhaps an orange robe, with cowboy boots? Here in Poona, Bodhie could expose his sweet, soft nature. He was the sweetest man, and Deepesh the handsomest, and they are my new friends, whom I love.

There were parties, and dinners, and groups. I joined a women's group to work on my high and low Moon energy. Yes, here in Poona everything is available. Love is always the focus.

A few days later, Bhagwan mentioned me in lecture. He spoke about one of my Darshans with him. I was exhilarated. This morning, as I explored my energy, I felt love in everyone's eyes. I looked into Suraj's eyes but I couldn't tell what he was feeling. I went away and cried. I told Bodhie this was the pain of falling in love.

There's nothing wrong with falling in love, Bhagwan told us that, often. Going through the wanting and then the teachings of the high moon drawing me back to remembering that if you get what you want that's fine, if you don't get what you want, that's fine also. I left the group in love with everyone.

'Bodhie, do you think I should work in the café now. Deeksha has asked me?'

'Veena, that's fabulous, she's a hard teacher, but you will learn so much. Come to dinner tomorrow, but quick, go and tell her now.'

'Thanks so much, see you tomorrow.'

I went home alone, shining with love. Suraj was not with me, but I didn't mind, in this loving mood it didn't matter who was with me. I just felt love through and through.

Next morning I went to Deeksha.

'Deeksha, I'm ready for some hard work.'

'That's good,' she said with her slight Italian accent. Deeksha is large and bossy. That's like an object lesson in front of me. If I'm not careful I will end up looking like her in a few years' time. That's a good meditation in itself, to keep remembering that I don't want to become any part of Deeksha.

I had written letters to Bhagwan before. After a week with Deeksha I wrote a desperate letter.

'Dear Bhagwan,

I just wanted to ask, are you really with me? Because Deeksha is beating me and strangling me and making fun of me and calling me names and pulling out every stop AND it hurts and sometimes I know I don't have enough trust in you - and her. I try to remember it's good for me – the fight grows less and less every day and still she says I'm impossible and negative and full of shit. Please, is there light at the end of the tunnel?

Every day I just do as I'm told, working, often silently and yet I'm still a fool, an idiot, all in the name of love? There are no men right now. I feel completely non-sexual, although maybe I just need to jump in? Madhuri says I'm always friends with all the sexy men.'

Love Deva Veena

I might as well send it, I thought. For once I didn't show it to anyone, I didn't want anyone to know how I felt. Although I'm realising it's probably all over my face!

At dinner the next night, Bodhie introduced me to Suman from Texas. Phew! They were hot, these Texans, what a drawling charmer. After yet another weary day with Deeksha in the café, we were going to meet and take a rickshaw into town for a mango pulp. I never really tasted mangoes until I came to Poona. This was heaven in a dish, Alphonso mango pulp served with cream on top, eaten by the grubby roadside. My favourite snack, people in London would be shocked.

Mango pulp and Suman soothed my soul. He's staying at the Blue Diamond and I'm invited back.

'Bodhie told me how gorgeous you are, but I don't think I'm ready to explore your gorgeousness yet. Thank you for a lovely evening, see you tomorrow.'

The pull to love is simmering underneath, I'm exploring what it feels like to be put on hold, complimented, then sent home!

'Thank you, Veena. See you tomorrow, we've got many more days to explore together, give me a hug.'

We parted sweetly at my gate at Sunder Lodge.

So the routine continued, Deeksha in the kitchen, friends in the evening, and Pari and Pradeepa usually around for a late night chat. What a great life, just sitting back and watching the peaks and troughs as Bhagwan had told me to do.

Bhagwan shared a Zen quote that said it better: 'Sitting quietly doing nothing, the spring comes and the grass grows all by itself.'

A trough was usually sitting in Greenfields eating too much. The curd set in small bowls served by the old-fashioned waiters, Indian waiters in bow ties. Healthy yes, necessary, no! Same with the creamy scrambled eggs, a reminder of England far away, because of course these waiters are a relic of the British Empire no doubt.

Vasudha and I were there often.

'So Veena, what's going on?'

'Well you have it easy, you're with Shanti.'

'Easy and Shanti, I would never have put them in the same breath.'

'Well now you mention it, he is very English and you're so very … fiery and Italian, how does that work?'

'Badly at times, he's so slow, so asleep, so prodding, I prod him all the time and then he sulks, bah! Bloody Englishmen. How's your Indian or your Texan or which one is it?'

'Mahesh, my sweetie, is the one, he should be coming here soon. But I don't know what will happen.'

'Just sit back and watch darling Veena, if you have the patience to be with these men.'

'Yes, these men bring out the four-year -old in me, and then my biggest battle, how do you Italians keep so thin, mind you, look at Deeksha.'

After that we started to laugh and laugh. Laughter is very cleansing, Sidarji the turbaned Sikh at the gate does a laughing meditation. We just laugh, his is the most infectious laugh and you feel it in your belly, it shakes your very being. This was a true belly laugh at the thought of roly poly Deeksha. Vasudha was probably the only slim Italian on the ashram, the love of pasta showed only too well on everyone else. I couldn't blame the pasta, I just blamed love, or lack of it.

'Let's go back now, Shanti will be waiting. Supper?'

'Yes please.'

We went outside to take a rickshaw to the River House.

MEETING THE MASTER

CHAPTER 15

Late that night after getting home from the River House I tried not to eat any more. But my four-year-old was raging … I thought of Mahesh and how wonderful I wanted to look.

'I'll write a letter to Bhagwan.'

> *Dear Bhagwan*
>
> *My four year old likes sweets and Deeksha's apple cake and ice cream and cashew nuts. My four year old wants to show off, my four year old is angry because people are stupid. My four year old wants to scream and yell – I don't know why, about lots of things. This is my last chance to be beautiful, stay beautiful, stay beautiful me. I know it, I don't want to hear it – don't need to ask. I know it, don't want to talk about it, don't need to destroy it. Doesn't matter, Deeksha's a big Momma, I'll be a small Momma please. Please help me to stop eating and destroying myself.*
>
> *All my love Veena*

I wanted to look beautiful for Mahesh, and impress Vinod, but from where I am standing, it's looking very hard.

I'm looking into a fragment of mirror I have in my sparse room. The silver from the back is starting to show through as I think to myself, 'perhaps I can lose a bit more by Monday, it's just two days away'. It was hard to remember the days.

'I just want to be beautiful and blow your mind Mahesh, and Vinod, and all your friends. I wanna make love with you, maybe Bhagwan will give you some sexual energy on his birthday.'

I'm thinking, as I smile to myself, do you know what: I don't care what you think of me – my four-year-old does, I don't.

Next morning I saw Gandha and her very proper English boyfriend

Sagar standing in line for lecture. I slipped into the line next to them. Behind Sagar's back we smiled and linked arms. He stood rod-like in front of us, his orange robe neat and uncreased, just skimming the floor, sandals clean and all correct. As we sat on the stone-cold floor Suman put his hand on my shoulder. I turned around.

'Hi sweetie, wanna meet tonight, come and find you later?' His eyes smouldered, and I nearly gasped aloud. It was like looking into Bhagwan's eyes, only not so frightening. Like eating and drinking something divine.

I steadied myself.

'Sure, see you later.'

Gandha smiled at me. Men loved me, my softness, my roundness, my small shining face with its hint of tan from my weeks in Poona. Mahesh was special, but then as Bhagwan had taught me, 'Just find someone no matter of choosing.'

A week later I had the chance to go to Darshan. I had to tell Bhagwan that I always fell in love with people who were not available and that I would like to fall in love with someone and have them fall in love with me.

Bhagwan said that unconsciously I did not really want to fall in love, so I chose people with whom my love could never be fulfilled. He said I chose people, not for themselves, but for their inaccessibility, and that if they became available I would drop the idea of pursuing them.

I said that either I tried to keep people away, or would simply go and grab at them, and that didn't work out either …

These are Bhagwan's words to me (May 6, 1977 and recorded in one of the Darshan books).

Bhagwan had sat up straight, looking me in the eye and in his soft, slightly accented voice had told me:

'Go and do that! Do something. And I'm not joking when I say 'go and do it.' Do it! I mean business.' He continued on in the chiding voice …

'You will be very happy once you get out of this circle you have created for yourself, this very self-destructive structure which is almost suicidal. If you don't love, you go on destroying your life. Love is life and through love, all other doors of prayer and God and everything is open. If the door of love is closed, you are left alone like a desert island and then there is no way to go anywhere. Then you get more and more fed up with yourself.

People take pride in being suicidal – drop that pride. Just look at the fact. And every human being is beautiful. Don't ask the impossible – just find someone who is available.

There are women I know who will become interested only in a married person, because then they can create trouble. If the person is not married they are not interested. That is their mathematics, if he were worth something, some other woman would have got hold of him before. Nobody has bothered about him – he is still a bachelor – so it certainly proves that he is not worth worrying about. At least he is not of the standard they would like.

Once the man has a woman, then other women start becoming interested. He must have something! They are more interested in creating jealousy in the other woman than love in the man. They are more interested in defeating the other woman. Their whole seduction, their whole coquetry, will be concerned with the woman; how they prove themselves to be better looking, more loving, more beautiful, more charming, and that the other woman is nothing. Once the woman has broken away from the man, they will not be interested in the man at all, the whole purpose is finished.

So never do that … that is ugly. And it is not going to help you because you are moving in a wrong direction. Find someone, or allow someone to find you.

It is good to play the game of hide and seek, but don't hide so much that the other gets fed up with the game and goes home! Then there will be no point.

Children play hide and seek but they always hide in such a way that the other can find them. It is never made almost impossible.

It is a challenge and they go on making noises so the other knows where they are. The other goes on playing the game of seeking them, knowing where they are. But if you hide so much that it becomes impossible to seek you, then the whole game is finished.

Nothing is wrong with you – it is just an old habit. It will melt with a little more understanding. Do something against it – that is the only way to break the habit.'

Chastened, I bowed at his feet and then staying on my knees, I shuffled away from Bhagwan, keeping my face towards him as I moved back into the circle. Gandha was in the circle, afterwards she hugged me.

'You don't know about Mahesh, just be there and see what happens.'

This was what he had spoken about in a lecture.

Morning lecture over, Gandha continued on into Lao Tzu House. She had a special position in the house of the Master. I thought she was special too.

That afternoon, Vasudha and I were going to the old sari market down by the river, near her house, the River House. Vashuda's clothes for export were made from old saris, India's gold.

'Wait until you go to Bombay, to the emporiums, and see the bales of silk and cottons, they are so beautiful. But I can't afford all that, that's why we're going here to the river.'

Old old women squatted over baskets of what looked like rags, down along the river bank. People looked at us curiously, after all we were two white women dressed in orange robes, the clothes of holy men who'd renounced all their worldly possessions, and we were scrabbling amongst the baskets of seeming rags. I watched while Vasudha found beautiful silks, satins, fine soft cottons. None of them were perfect but it didn't matter. We would wash them, carefully, and lay them out along the river bank to dry. The local women washed them in the river, not sure if we would do that.

'Rich Indian women have thrown these out and bought more, so now we're lucky, helps my business.'

'How wonderful. You're so clever Vasudha. What will I do, my money will run out soon. I'll probably just have to ring home and ask them to wire more, if they will. It may be time to move house soon, find something cheaper.'

'You know I would ask you to live at the River House, but I don't think with Shanti ...'

'It's OK. I know you would. I wish I could buy a room in the ashram, but I don't think I'm quite surrendered enough yet!' Such a strange word to use, I hadn't even known what it meant a few weeks ago, and now I felt I might be on the path. But a room was a few thousand rupees, I didn't have that either.

'Do you think I should sleep with Suman if he asks me?' I inquire.

'Bhagwan told you to choose, so go choose, and enjoy.'

'You're right, if he wants to, he might just want to talk.'

'Veena, are you losing your touch?'

'No just practicing whilst my Anthony is away, my Mahesh.'

We struggled along with a huge bale of secondhand saris. I put Vasudha into a rickshaw and made my way back to the ashram. It was a stifling afternoon, not the hottest season yet, but I sat well back in the rickshaw so I wouldn't get caught in the hot breeze. I'd got used to feeling hot, and sometimes thirsty, and everyone said drink, drink, drink all the time.

Suman was hanging by the gate smoking beedies, deep in conversation with Bodhie. I felt good today, in spite of the long bumpy ride back in the rickshaw.

'Let's meet at 8pm' Suman told me.

'Let's, where?'

'I'm still at the Blue Diamond, meet you outside.'

'You know they hate us sannyasins, please don't leave me standing there too long.'

'Would I, you beautiful creature? See you later.'

'Bye Bodhie, bye Suman, see you later.'

Quick wave and I left to make myself beautiful. More beautiful, I corrected myself in my head.

The evening air in Poona was delicious, I had cleaned and washed and brushed up for Suman, and put on something soft and floaty. He looked me up and down appreciatively.

Later, we made love under the mosquito net in Suman's room at the Blue Diamond. We stroked and caressed, I was hungry but so was Suman so we fed each other with lust, and in my case, love. Everything for me was a craving and nothing was quite satisfying.

We stood and washed each other afterwards in the shower. I felt stoned, intoxicated, and Suman's eyes shone. Was this what Bhagwan meant me to do?

DINNER WITH
THE MOVIE STAR

CHAPTER 16

Today Mahesh was coming to the ashram with Vinod. Gandha would have to escape from Sagar. Bless him, dear old Sagar, everyone including me, wondered what she saw in the crusty old English guy. Did he protect her? She told me she had never cheated before, but Vinod was too much of a catch.

First, there was another day of Deeksha to be endured. I set out the breakfast on the counter and was then ordered outside to clean the tables. I was just clearing away the plates and cups when a tall, handsome man approached and sat down.

'Do I need to help myself?' he asked me in ringing English tones.

'Yes, that would be good,' and I showed him where to go.

Varag from the office who is normally so calm, rushed up exclaiming: 'Oh my God, do you know who that is?'

'No, who?' I asked.

'It's that movie star from England.'

'Who?'

'Terence Stamp.'

'I've heard of him, wow.'

Varag rushed away to tell more people, I took one last look, he was mesmerizing, compelling and charismatic. He turned at that moment and caught me looking. I blushed slightly and moved away towards the kitchen to prevent an outburst from Deeksha. Deeksha probably wouldn't care if the Pope arrived, work is work.

Soon the girls from the office came to fuss over him and take him to his quarters. How intriguing I thought, but my mind was more on my own Indian movie man.

I had no idea what time Mahesh and Vinod would arrive and in the searing heat it was hard to stay looking good all day. They would no doubt step from their air-conditioned limousine looking immaculate and handsome, even my darling, different as he was from the handsome movie star all the Indians adored. It's nice. I thought to myself, Vinod and Gandha get all the attention, so for once I can have Mahesh all to myself. A few people knew who he was, but not all.

I walked down to the gate again, for the third or fourth time, I'd lost count. There was a small crowd, and there was Mahesh.

'Veena,' he cried, arms outstretched. 'Veena, come quickly, we need music, sunsets, falling leaves, Lara's theme.'

'That is such a sad movie.'

'But it's my favourite, sorry sweetie.' Indians have such old fashioned terms of endearment.

Mahesh and I linked arms. Mahesh did not stay with Vinod anymore, certainly not since that first night, he stayed at Mobos hotel. Not as smart as Vinod but private, so we had our own room, together.

I loved his brown body, sometimes when he wasn't with me I would imagine the imprint of it on mine, his weight as he lay on me sometimes. If I closed my eyes I could smell the sweat. Oh my God I loved him so much, yes, another unavailable man, was I taking note of anything Bhagwan told me? But, when we embraced, the whole world disappeared, and we were only there for each other. It was better than the movies he made. This was a movie he made with his little plump English girl.

I had told Deeksha I could not work that afternoon. Deeksha did not seem to give much attention to matters of the heart, so I was economical with my words.

'Just a friend from Bombay you know, I said I would meet him. I'll do a bit extra next week.'

'Extra? What you do is never enough, get out of here.' She patted me on my bottom, as I fled.

So now we headed for the Blue Diamond where we would sit together and spend time looking over the script he had brought with him. We sat in the coffee bar, I felt encased in his warmth as we sat close, not touching, not caressing, just having a mundane conversation about not much. If only I could have captured this moment, on celluloid, forever.

As we sat there, Bodhie appeared in front of us.

'Hey Veena, we're going out with the movie star for dinner, do you want to come?'

'Oh yes, I'd love to. Will you come Mahesh, please?'

Mahesh shook his head. But still I dragged him over to the bar where Bodhie and the others were sitting. Deepesh, Leena, Madhuri, now known by her new nickname 'Mudpie' were joined by Bodhie and Terence Stamp the actor. Terence sat at the bar, a stern upright figure. He was now dressed in green, softer and less conspicuous, he told us, his enraptured audience, as he sipped a soda. I laughed as he told jokes, stealing quick looks into those big blue eyes. Mahesh sat behind me, with his head in my shoulder.

Deepesh introduced Mahesh to Terence as a leading Indian movie director. Mahesh seemed to just want to hide more, he buried his head deeper into my shoulder.

This amused Deepesh.

'I'm just going to walk Mahesh back to the ashram, you're not leaving yet are you?'

'No dearest Veena, of course, we'll wait for you,' Deepesh told me.

Mahesh and I walked back to the ashram together, along the busy main road, into Koregan Park, dusty and unmade. The corner house was glittering, silhouetted by fairy lights for a forthcoming wedding.

'Veena,' he scolded, 'Veena, you're just like my daughter, you show off when there's new people.'

'How old is your daughter?'

'Four.'

'Well if I'm four, you must be too.'

We danced along Koregan Park, happy and loving, at peace. I dropped him at the gate.

Mahesh said wistfully, rather like a small boy: 'Off to meet the movie star then? Prefer him to me?'

'Of course not silly, hug me, kiss me. Please come back soon.'

I skipped back down the road, careful to avoid any potholes. I felt a pang, a touch of emptiness, a missing piece as we parted and went our separate ways.

But this was an adventure, with other people I loved. We were going to a restaurant down Laxmi Road, across the river, strange places, furthest journey for many months. I felt happy, energised, cool, mellow. Off to dinner.

At dinner I sat opposite the movie star. He revealed to us that Bhagwan had given him a new name, Veeten. This name felt easier, as I sat opposite him trying not to look into his mesmerising eyes. But I was just drawn in. I tried not to look with longing, but when I did look he matched my gaze and held it. He was complicit in the game. What a handsome powerful man.

Usually I was not mindful of the food I ate, but now I was influenced and guided by his austerity. No, no tartar sauce. No ice cream, no, not even from someone else's spoon. This guy made me forget food!

Veeten stepped outside for a pan, with Deepesh. I had tried it, and hated the bitter paste rolled up in leaves which delighted the men. But I went outside with them anyway, and linked arms with both of them while they chewed, I was thrilled, and glowing, in the dark.

I'm with all my special friends, Deepesh and Leena, full of love,

Deepesh wearing his be-dragoned jacket, beautiful Bodhie, and Madhuri who had been intent upon eating. Madhuri loved her food. I had been more intent upon Veeten.

After the meal I managed to manoeuvre myself into a rickshaw with Veeten, still clutching his arm. We laughed and chatted, about Bhagwan and nose rings, and Bhagwan, and more Bhagwan. Veeten had many questions.

'What are you doing here?' I asked him.

'It's part of my journey,' he answered, 'just part of my journey.'

At my house I jumped out, he jumped out too and kissed me goodbye on both cheeks. He asked my name again.

'It's Veena.'

'Goodnight Veena.'

I floated into bed. Drunk with Veeten, Mahesh on my mind. I fell fast asleep after a beautiful day.

BELOVED BENITA'S

CHAPTER 17

I have a new friend, well a new old friend. Anam - Hugh as I first knew him, came from North London too, near my home there.

Anam was a wow with the ladies, actually with the fellows too! But I wasn't enticed by him at all. So he was my friend, my confidante, my sarcastic critic and fellow wit!

Anam had a room in the ashram, I had been impressed initially, thinking he had money. But I learned that he was a designer and in return for his hard work designing a diary, the Sannyas newspaper and other design projects, they had given him a room in Krishna house.

As my money got less and less I started to look for a new place to live. We were strolling out of morning lecture, enjoying a few minutes before work began.

'Why don't you come and live at beloved Benita's?'

'What the hell is beloved Benita's?'

'My girlfriend lives there, Benita is an Indian lady with some spare rooms. I think she likes to think she's rather refined and middle-class, but she's not really. Her mouth is red from chewing pan all the time. She has a servant girl who tidies your room, God knows if she snoops as well. But I like it.'

He could be very arch, and pompous when he spoke like that. I began to see the male point of view.

'Well, why don't you ask her?'

'OK will do.' We're sitting on a wall outside the ashram and the Indians are starting to look at us suspiciously, jeering a little.

'This is unpleasant, let's go inside.'

'Good idea.'

Just then the girls came by.

'Bye Anam.'

'Bye Veena.'

I linked arms with the girls, and we left Anam sitting in the scorching sun.

Madhuri said: 'When you've finished slaving for Deeksha, we're going up to the roof, but be sure to bring some popai.'

'Popai? What for?'

'Just bring it, we'll show you.'

'OK, see you later.'

The morning passed quietly. I had learned how to do what Deeksha wanted and avoid fuss and telling off. I also discovered that Deeksha had a soft side. I found out about this one day when I was crying in a corner over something. Deeksha had come over and comforted me, clasping me to her huge bosom, then she'd given me food. Good, but not quite perfect.

When no-one was looking I slid a piece of popai into a napkin and sped up to the roof.

Up on the roof all the girls were laid out in the sun, the burning afternoon sun, with popai smeared all over their faces and any other parts which could be bared to the sun.

'What does that do, besides make you unbearably sticky?'

'Conditions the skin and gets you browner,' Madhuri answered from near the ground, through screwed up eyes.

'Oh well, let's try'. I smeared my face, it didn't feel unpleasant, just very sticky.

After probably 10 minutes in the burning sun I gave up and sat in the shadows. Someone had brought The Times of India up to read. It's a broadsheet, with maybe only four to six pages. None of us knew the date that day, so we didn't know if it was last week's or last month's news.

'Oh my God, look, Elvis died.'

For a minute we were all lost in thought, united by our memory of the great man. Whether you loved his music or not, it was a sad moment.

I was starting to feel a little queasy, must be the heat I thought to myself.

'I'm going down into the shade.'

'Bye, see you later,' they chorused.

By 5 o'clock I felt very bad, and it was then that Anam came to find me to tell me the news that beloved Benita had a bed to offer me, and I could move immediately.

'Come on, come on, let's do it now,' Anam urged.

'I don't feel great.'

Anam was being kind. 'I'll help you, you can't have that much stuff. Let's get a rickshaw.'

We took the rickshaw round to Sunder Lodge and loaded it up, Anam took a second rickshaw and drove in front, guiding mine, which was loaded up to the roof.

I felt so groggy I didn't take much notice of where we were going, I paid and stumbled up the stairs with my mostly orange belongings.

'Thank you, Anam.'

'Thank you, sweetie, nice to see you here.'

'I'm just going to collapse on the bed, please tell Benita I will speak with her later.'

'Will do,' he said over his shoulder as he left.

But later never came as my head stayed down on the pillow all night.

Anam stayed over at Benita's with Gopi that night. He put his head round my door to discover I was a delicate shade of yellow, hepatitis had struck.

'What will I do?'

'Nothing, you'll have to stay in bed. I'll send Amrit, the English doctor, just sleep.'

Amrit came, and went. I was so groggy I could barely remember him being there or what he said. He wanted me to take some strange medicine from an ayurvedic doctor. I was too weak to argue, and I didn't really care. If only they would let me sleep. My food was to be boiled vegetables and dahi.

'What's dahi?' I asked weakly from my sick bed. Thank God I had moved to beloved Benita's. There was a wonderful fan above my bed and with closed windows, I had created a cool darkness in which to sleep. I did not even need a mosquito net, which had become part of life since living in India. How lucky.

'Dahi is just very thin curd.'

'Not like the gorgeous stuff from Greenfield's?

'Absolutely not,' Anam had retorted. 'You can't have any fats, your liver won't stand it. Look on the bright side, you might lose pounds.'

I closed my eyes weakly, if I survive, yes I might, but who would be there to see it?

'Veena, I'm going to the ashram, I'll tell everyone about you. Sleep. Benita is fine, her girl will feed you. See you later.'

'Thank you, Anam,' I said as my eyes shut and I lay against the pillow. 'Thank you, what would I have done without you?'

'Don't worry. In a few days I'll bring you some visitors.'

'Not yet.'

'No, not yet.'

THE 'OTHER' GIRLFRIEND

CHAPTER 18

I was so lucky. After three days of sleep I awoke refreshed, and weak and wobbly, and missing Mahesh.

'I could write to him could I not?' I quizzed Anam.

'Yes, do you have an address?'

'Well I was wondering, do you suppose you could go to the ashram office and see if they will give it to you?'

'For you darling, anything.'

I blew kisses as he left the apartment. It was true, I was beginning to lose weight, eating only the purest of food. If anyone crossed me, my temper flared up at once. No food to hold anything back I realised. A little scary with my fiery temper!

I had lots of time on my hands, and alone I began to think about England and my family. Part of my reason for coming to Poona had been to put some distance between me and my mother. We'd always had a difficult relationship and this way it was confined to letters. I felt I'd always been a disappointment to my mother. God knows what she had wanted me to be. But, whatever it was, she had not shown any interest or support and when I got my first job, a teaching job, she criticised. So I didn't really know what would have fulfilled her dreams, let alone mine.

Other people had come to escape their parents and their disappointments. To love, find love and surrender, with the guru.

Should I write and tell her I'm ill? But if I do that I know what will happen. I'll get phone calls to come home, I will write, and use it as an opportunity to ask for some money. Not great, I know, but necessary.

I had arrived with money from the teaching job in London, my first, and probably my last, job it felt like! My money had lasted well, but was now running out. It was very cheap in Poona, and working with Deeksha at least provided free meals. But sometimes it was a delicate balance.

The day passed slowly. Madhuri and Bodhie were coming to see me later. That got me through the day.

However, Bodhie arrived later, alone.

'I'm so glad you're here, I've been thinking about England. It seems a million miles away, but still depressing. Do you think about your family?'

'Try not to, but they worry about me sometimes.'

He pulled a bottle of beer out of his bag and took off the cap. 'Hey, how can you drink that in front of me when you know I'll probably never be able to touch alcohol again. That's not nice!'

'Hey Veena, touchy,' he said in his wonderful Texan drawl. 'You never know, you'll probably be able to drink again soon.'

Anam barged in just then. 'Veena, they don't have his address.'

'Oh my God, I hate this, it's not fair.'

I lay back on the pillow, overexerted.

'Hey Anam, let's go and get some food,' Bodhie said, not realising how left out it made me feel.

'Great, bye Veena, see you later.'

'Bye guys,' I gave them a smile from my pillow. I know it was a watery smile, it felt watery.

All that time alone gave me time to think, and resent. I began to really think about Mahesh and the relationship we had. The first time we'd met, that was enough, so fulfilling. It was unreal and thrilling and crazy, and now, without you, I feel insecure, I told myself, or did I just feel insecure about everything?

Then when you come to the ashram you go off to be with the guys. Are you pretending not to be with me? Must it always be like this? I know who I like, and then we start running and pretending.

'I want to play, have fun and love you, and walk into the sunset – if it's bullshit it's no more bullshit than anything else ever is - I just can't wait forever here and I don't feel like running away so's just not to be here when you come. Oh that I should be so smart and cool like all those Bombay ladies, who look down their manicured fingers and feign boredom. I beg your pardon they are bored – I'm not, not yet.'

I had said the last part out loud!! I looked round, the fan merely kept turning, the blinds flapped ever so slightly. No, my passion had no effect on the walls and windows.

I fell asleep, and dreamt of Mahesh.

I was feeling better these days, and staying in was hard. Anam was as attentive as he could be, it varied according to his social commitments which I discovered were many! But he brought me Bhagwan tapes and I lay back in my bed and listened. It brought me some peace as the words flooded over me. Particular things resonated. Bhagwan spoke about being an empty space and letting things flood in. Was this why I now had hepatitis after two years in India, was this yet another meditation, a look to see how 'enlightened' I am getting?

'Unless you accept yourself as a blessing, unless you accept and welcome yourself, unless you accept yourself in deep gratitude, unless you love yourself you will never become an overflowing energy.'

I sighed. I am trying. Loving this ever-shrinking Veena is easier.

In two days' time I'm going to the ashram. Amrit, the English doctor had given it the OK and I'm so looking forward to it.

The day came, it felt like the thinnest day of the year, I was full of desiring and dreaming. Not that Bhagwan would approve. I felt floaty after the hepatitis, light headed, and the heat seemed very intense after being under the fan for so long. I had dressed carefully, to show off my new figure in a shirt and loose trousers, orange of course. People had started to wear 'near' colours, but I loved vibrant orange. I tied them carefully with a chiffon scarf round my waist.

Anam held my arm after discourse. I'm going to do a little work, and then take it easy. Then, at lunch, I catch a glimpse of Mahesh, with a beautiful Indian woman, and Vinod too.

They walked over and said 'hi.'

I tried to open the conversation, but they carried on walking, so I did too.

Inwardly, I fumed … 'Doesn't look like you're looking for me, Mahesh!' I carried on with my work.

At 6 o'clock as I was approaching the main gate, I saw Mahesh was there with Vinod.

'Mahesh, what are you doing here?'

He stretched out his arms to me, and shouted out my name. 'My little fatty bum bum, come here and let me see you.'

'But I'm not,' I cried out, dancing a little, punching the air, drinking in his energy.

'Veena, you've reduced,' Vinod exclaimed.

'Yes, I was trying to tell you at lunchtime, when you asked me how I was, but you didn't wait for the answer.' I was so cross, I'd spent the afternoon swearing under my breath about bloody movie stars, which gave me loads of energy to clean the floors, yes I was back at cleaning, for now.

Vinod laughed. Seems he didn't pick up how rude I had just been, and even if he did, he was a polite Indian gentleman.

'Veena, I'm here with Parveen. Would you like to come for a drink with us at the Blue Diamond?'

'Who's Parveen?' I asked, with as much dignity as I could muster.

'She's a movie star and very special friend. Like you.' he saved himself as my face started to fall.

'Come on all my girls, let's go.'

I studied Parveen out of the corner of my eye. She was very beautiful and seemed very comfortable with Mahesh. There was nothing I could do and it was better to be there, than not I figured. Even without meeting Parveen. I knew I was sharing Mahesh, and until now, I had not wanted to ever see the competition.

Still, the sight of him made my heart soar. What a wonderful first day out of bed, even if it was not going to end back in bed with my sweetie.

THE TAJ MAHAL HOTEL
BOMBAY

CHAPTER 19

Mahesh had gone early the next day, with Parveen and Vinod. It had been very hard for me. I had felt so intoxicated with myself, cleansed and clear after the hepatitis.

Now I had long days without Mahesh, so I struck up acquaintance with various cute men. Mahesh remained steadfastly on my mind, as much as I tried to get rid of the thought of him. He made no contact.

One day, a German photographer arrived on assignment for Stern magazine. I hung around and we started talking.

'Would you like to join me in Bombay?' George asked.

'Wow, how long for?'

'Just a few days, I'm staying at the Taj.'

I took an inward gasp, The Taj. I'd heard of Bombay's premier hotel and it had been so long since I'd had any luxury. Beloved Benita's was comfortable, but not much more.

'George, I'd love that.'

'Good, then pack a few things and we can leave.'

Inside I'm thrilled, I sense another adventure, so with a few goodbyes I get into the car with George. I knew it was a smart hotel, and with only my orange clothes, I would stand apart from the smart Bombay ladies, apart in not an altogether good way. But, I thought to myself, I have an inner glow, I must have something for George to have asked me to join him.

The journey was long and dusty, three hours of Indian roads where the driving was erratic and noisy. If anyone got in the way the driver just honked his horn but kept driving, never slowing down.

The best, the only way to be was to relax, take a deep breath and sit back. There did not seem to be as many accidents as you might expect, so something about it worked, specially as we arrived in Bombay unscathed.

It was quite shocking to be in a large city after being in the countryside. There were beggars everywhere, beggars with children, beggars pulling other beggars on little carts. The beggars on the carts had limbs missing; arms, legs. It was horrible, I sat back in the car shuddering. Then we pulled up outside the magnificent hotel. We got out and grabbed our bags and then had to push past more beggars on the front steps, the contrast between the 'haves' and the 'have nots' was shocking. A turbaned man greeted us and we were ushered into the marbled reception with its icy air conditioning.

George booked in and we're ushered to a seating area where we are served coconut juice, served from the coconut with the green husk still on it.

I tried to sit in a sophisticated manner as if this happened to me every day. It was worth being there just to see how people lived, people with money in India. There was a huge divide between the very rich, successful Indians, high achieving and ambitious for not only themselves, but their offspring as well - and the poor unfortunate beggars outside in the streets.

Small problem. I'm a little alarmed at the prospect of sleeping with George, and I'm wondering if I can get rid of him and get a room for myself.

George had taken a room for us on the 11th Floor. As we got upstairs to the room, George said, 'I'm tired from the journey, if you want to go down and look around, see the pool, the coffee shop, I'm fine with that, I'll see you later.'

'Wow, thanks George' I bent over and gave him a sort of affectionate caress. A quick look in the mirror, smoothed my hair, shook a little of the dust from the road off my clothes and took a fast-moving lift ride to the ground floor.

Down in the coffee shop I sat on a stool and ordered a sweet lassi. Just then three Arabs, two in robes and head dresses, came and sat nearby. I tried not to look at them, but one of them, who could have come straight out of Lawrence of Arabia, caught my eye.

'Hello, my name is Mohamed, would you like to join us?'

'I'd love to.'

I take a metaphorical picture from the corner of the ceiling, something I'm familiar with.

I'm dressed in orange sitting in the restaurant at the Taj Mahal hotel in Bombay with three Arab gentlemen, two in full Arab headgear.

This is what the management saw. I didn't.

'Would you like to join us for dinner?' asks Mohamed.

'Love to.'

Oh my God, I'm smitten, these men, all married, have come from the Arab Emirates to meet women, drink wine, do all the forbidden things, and here I am ready to play.

After dinner, Mohamed and I are left alone, Dr. Lamb retires to his room.

'Do you think I should get you your own room here in the hotel?' Mohamed asks me.

'I would really like that,' I say, holding my breath. I can't see anything wrong with that, after all George was just the vehicle to get me here, I had not promised him anything, and besides, he had an assignment, I tell myself. 'Thank you' I'm still holding my breath.

Next thing I remember, I'm waking up in my beautiful room on the 17th floor of the Taj. You stayed until dawn Mohamed, and I slept until nine. I lay and listened to Stevie Wonder. I had not been in such luxury for so long, ashram life was sparse.

It was a beautiful room with its red curtains, red carpet and beautiful bed with big fluffed white pillows. Pillows, I'd been sleeping on a rolled up blanket for a pillow. The bathtub was beautiful. I'd cleaned a couple of bathrooms in the ashram a week or two ago, not quite so big and luxurious, now I was laid out in one with oiled water swirling around me. All I had to do was lay there and the dirt would float off, but hopefully not your scent, Mohamed.

Mohammed Ahli, the third gentleman, had invited me for breakfast at his table. Was every Arab called Mohammed? He asked me: 'please my dear Veena, please come and meet with me in my suite at 2.30.'

Ha, you can't buy me. I'm such a fool, they'd all bought me, but my eyes were so full of stars I couldn't see.

I didn't go, instead I went for a swim in the beautiful indoor pool. Mohamed was watching the young girls swim. I thought I caught a glimpse of George in the distance from my comfortable padded lounger. I pulled the white fluffy towel up higher.

Another dinner with all three and then Mohamed and I, giggling like school kids, fled to my 'red room.'

This was to be my last night. Next morning I was summoned to the hotel office.

'Madam, we believe you are here on business, you are soliciting men, we see you have a room paid for by one of our guests, we suggest you leave. If you leave now we will not pursue this matter, thank you for your co-operation.'

I sat in shock, of course. Suddenly I can see why they think this. I muster as much dignity as I can and rush out of the room to look for Mohamed. But they have spoken to him before me, and told him I'm a prostitute and he, having a reputation to preserve, has paid for the room and closed the account. Eventually, I found him in the restaurant.

'I'm so sorry if I did anything wrong.'

'You didn't, but what I'd like to do is buy you a ticket to go home to your family. Stop this crazy life you have in Poona.'

'I can't let you do that. Besides, I'm happier in Poona than with my family, believe me, they don't want me.'

But I'm not that proud, or stupid, and he pays for my car back to Poona, and I even have enough money to stop on the way and buy cakes. So when I arrive back, I'm the toast of the town, and curiously enough I haven't thought about Mahesh for the past few days, even though I was in his home city. So close, yet so far.

Back at the ashram I write Mohamed a letter, in reply to his earlier one:

Mohamed, thank you so much for your letter, I wrote another one to you at the Taj Mahal – perhaps the manager is enjoying it even now! Doesn't matter, hope everything is well with you and your wife.

I cried when I got your letter – I had been so very happy in Bombay, I couldn't understand what TERRIBLE thing I had done to make you so angry.

From what happened we both learnt a lesson in trust – me that I should have left for Poona as you told me even without knowing why. YOU – you should have told me, did you believe this story? Even the note signed Elizabeth (I did not read it) was NOT from me.

You know in those magic days you were the only person who mattered for me. It would even have been easy to go with Juma and Mohamed Ahli – but I didn't and didn't want to. I loved you as soon as I looked into your beautiful eyes. I don't want you, I just love you – don't be afraid of my words just understand. But next time tell everything, and then I could have told you it was lies – you knew anyway!

You knew I was only with you.

Much love

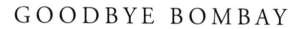

GOODBYE BOMBAY

CHAPTER 20

Back in the ashram amongst my friends I kept thinking of Bhagwan's words about being loved and loving myself.

'I'm not sure I'm following what he told me,' I said to myself.

I whiled away the long hours back in the kitchen with Deeksha, thinking of love and Mahesh. Not much joy there, knowing Mahesh was both rapture and torture all at the same time.

Mohamed's words about going back to England also rang in my ears.

One day, I decided it was time to leave for England. Mahesh visited the ashram and I told him my plan.

'Good idea, would you like to stay at my apartment in Bombay when you leave?'

I nodded.

'And spend a day with me?'

Tears welled up.

'You know I would.'

I packed my bags, I didn't have much, just orange robes and dresses, said a few goodbyes and went to the station to take the train to Bombay. It was hot and steamy weather, and then, just outside the station, the train broke down. I watched all the people clamber out and walk along the tracks; the old men in dhotis, the women and children. I climbed out of the carriage and followed them, holding an umbrella to keep off the burning sun in one hand while carrying my bags in the other. Quite a feat!

I had become so Indian.

My day with Mahesh was like a dream. He took me to hear Krishnamurti speak, we sat on the ground and he gave me a grey shawl to wrap round myself as it was cooler at dusk. It was strange wearing another colour. The nearly night air was full of mystical words and cawing birds. At any moment it seemed as if Lara's theme would play. In the presence of Krishnamurti, and Mahesh also wrapped in a grey shawl, all I felt was love, and for a moment, contentment.

The evening was less magical. Parveen joined us and he took us both to see 'The Duchess and the Dirtwater Fox.' I don't remember much about the movie, Mahesh sat with a hand on each of us, I was more intent on watching them than the screen.

Then he went home with Parveen, whilst I went home alone to his luxury apartment with only the manservant asleep on the mat inside his front door for company. What was it about him that made him so lovable to all us women?

Next day, he took me lovingly to the airport.

I wanted to be cross with him and then he told me: 'Veena, you are very special, you are a special woman. I'm sorry if I've treated you badly, you deserved more.'

'Go Mahesh, you'll make me cry. Goodbye.'

We kissed, onlookers stopped to see what the famous movie director was doing. To me, he was just Mahesh, my cuddly, romantic man.

Back in London the Mahesh story wasn't over.

I became Elizabeth again, the nose ring is gone and I'm a suburban housewife. Five years later, I'm married and have children. I type interviews for TV programmes and care for my children.

Late one night, I'm typing an interview in which an MP (Member of Parliament) from Bombay speaks of Mahesh. Mahesh! All that longing stirs, I've never forgotten him. I wonder to myself, could I get in touch with him?

I write a note to the MP, just addressed with his name and Maharastra, Bombay. Inside, I enclose another short note to Mahesh. I put it in the post.

He replies:

Hi! Beautiful – it was really nice reading your letter. As days go by – I get more and more certain that my life is imitating a B grade Hindi movie – full of twists and turns –melodrama- all that stuff a movie is made of. Now look at the way you got to hear about me, and there I was shooting when Miss Green suddenly springs up and talks.

Damn it you should have at least written a few abuses to me – after all that was no way to treat a lady the last time we parted.

You have confirmed again what I always thought of you, you are a sweetheart. I gave up Rajneesh about two and a half years ago. I have been through a lot. Parveen had a mental breakdown, I tried but she was never quite the same again. I am no longer with her, I know I can be of more use from further away.

It's been excruciating.

I came to London last year. I was there about 15 days. I would come again soon. Will you mother me? Take care of me, fuss over me, fuck with me? Feed me, bathe me?

Let me know your number I could talk to you, Bombay to London is direct dial.

That's all sweetie. Nothing profound to say yeah! I do feel great affection for that girl Veena as the past flashes   through my head.

Thanks for everything. Write again.

Lots of love, etc.

I am transported back to India, to my sweetie, to that crazy moment in my life.

Three weeks later the phone rings.

'How are you? Are you still my beautiful girl?'

I sigh and hold in my stomach as if somehow he can see me.

'Here, let me give you my office number.' My husband is hovering in the room as if sensing something. I take the number, reluctantly say 'Goodbye,' and hang up the phone.

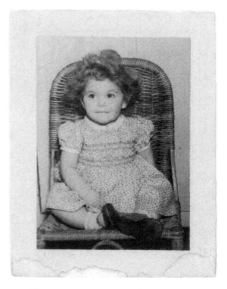

The princess is born   Ruminating on life already

At the beach in Birchington eating ice cream.
Developing a lifetime habit

In my Princess Anne coat in the park

My first – and last – modelling job

Named and shamed. Clothes
handmade by the nanny

Our little Lord Fauntleroy moment in blue velvet

1960 Christmas at the Ambassador's Hotel Bournemouth

In my "orange" attire. Yes, I knew Ma Anand Sheela
(Wild Wild Country on Netflix)

Getting ready for the 1982 New York Marathon

1980s wedding fashion

P·R·A·C·T·I·C·A·L

PARENTING

£1

JULY 1990

How to hug, handle and hold your baby

PREGNANT AND IN THE KITCHEN
Freeze-ahead recipes for after the birth

SURPRISE BIRTHS
'I never thought it would happen that way!'

SPECIAL SECTION

STRANGER DANGER!
Report on risks, plus practical protection plan for your child

PLUS
- Facts of life for kids
- Bottlefeeding basics
- Healthcare: children's skin

EXTRA
Choices in Childcare
8-PAGE SPECIAL

Grin and bare it: Georgia Neville, 18 months, shows off her smooth skin. See how your baby can have perfect skin on page 17

Cover girl Georgia aged 2

Jacob aged 8 at work. He didn't want to do it,
but had a great time and got paid

Me, Philip and his beloved Ma at Georgia's Bat Mitzvah

Family fun in France! They haven't washed for a week!
Best part of camping

West End debut, Jacob aged 8 in
'Waiting for Godot.' Nerve wracking
in the wings for me

BBC TV series, Georgia
aged 8 in 'No Sweat,'
playing the naughty sister.
Typecasting?

Proud Grandma at Georgia's Bat Mitzvah

At my mother's 89th/90th birthday party.
Look how well we scrub up! A slim year post-divorce

Me and Jackie Mason in Miami, Oy Vay!

Sisters-in-law in togas at 'The' 50th Birthday Party

New Year, new love? No, give me thrills

In her second dispatch from the dating scene, ***Elizabeth Green*** *— sister of Topshop boss Sir Philip — finds love. She's not sure she wants it, though*

IMAGINE THE scene. It's New Year's Eve, another bleak day and night ahead. My children are getting ready for the big night, although my daughter has my attitude. "It's just another night out — what a fuss," she says.

My plans for the evening were set when Karen, an old (single) friend, got in touch after many months with the offer of a party in Edgware. I dithered and dallied until deciding it was better than staying at home alone.

We set off on the journey across North London, hampered only by www.aa.com's directions and the borough of Barnet's lack of road signs.

the close off the main street and went in.

Inside, we had to walk across the room with all eyes — particularly male ones — on us, to put our coats down while smiling weakly at people. Our hostess had told us there would be men — desperate men at that. If we girls are desperate, we hide it better, of course.

A Jewish gathering, and I didn't know anyone; was this a first? However, the man leaning against the wall in the kitchen looked very familiar — not handsome, but recognisable. I knew I'd seen him before. "What do you do for a living?" I asked. I knew if he said "wedding cars" he was the one on *JDate* who had arranged to walk my dogs with me, got flu and never rang again.

"Wedding cars," he said.

"We were going to dog-walk," I accused.

He looked at me. His eyes lit up. God was good — here was a second chance. I think his evening had just got better, too.

Karen found some people interested in ceroc and danced. I chatted — not just with Mr Wedding Cars, but with Mr Blue Check Shirt too. None of it was an effort.

At midnight we all popped party poppers, sipped sparkling wine and sang *Auld Lang Syne*. When I got home I put on the TV to try to recapture the

Elizabeth Green: "Why don't I want the ones who want me?"

fireworks I'd left recording. Bad idea: fell asleep, another year ahead.

New Year's Day. Mr Wedding Cars and I walk the dogs, have lunch together with my 17-year-old son and we all go

he's in love. Instant family heaven for a lonely man.

Mr Wedding Cars lives alone and had planned a solitary new year's day till we came along. Trouble is, I'm not

to be loved and adored and cuddled," he tells me. Don't we all, I muse.

"So, are you moving in this week or next?" I ask.

"Next," he says.

How funny, and how not. It seems he's fallen hard. But here's the question: why don't I want the ones that want *me*? How easy would it be to invite him for lunch and have him never leave. I know people who've done that with their new internet loves. But, I tell him, something stops me.

Am I spoilt? Ungrateful? Or just unleashed?

Mr Blue Check Shirt just rang to ask me for a drink, and someone else wants me to come for lunch on Monday. I think I'm becoming a serial luncher. How many lunches can one girl have? Many, many — I deserve it.

Late the next day, my daughter rang to see how my evening went. I mentioned Mr Wedding Cars.

"What's he like?" she asks (we always compare notes).

"Well, you know, he's kind of funny looking, but cute," I say.

"Just like our dogs," she replies.

Bad girl, but yes. I'm ready for excitement, adventure, love and thrills. I don't want dog-like devotion. Not yet.

For details of Elizabeth Green's Trusting Love relationship courses, email elizabeth

THEJC.COM

THE JEWISH CHRONICLE
13 JUNE 2008

DATING DIARY ELIZABETH GREEN

He told me I was 'the one'. You can never trust emails

The sister of Sir Philip Green learns that internet romances can only lead to heartache

I WAS brought up in a cold climate, and I don't mean the weather. Having survived the angst of my teenage years, I have been on a quest for love ever since.

Now, a year after my divorce, I yearn to find someone who can't live without me. Has this impaired my judgement, made me rash and crazy? With my heart on my sleeve, I've become fair game, and what a game it turned out to be.

It was a wet Sunday night and I was taking a last, longing look at *JDate* on my computer before going to bed. Questions ran round my head: "Is this box ever going to deliver a wonderful man or just another sad loser?" Mind you, does that make *me* a sad loser for looking?

And then the email dropped into my inbox. "CEO of American company coming to live and work in London seeks lovely lady. You look lovely, can we email?" I admit it — my head was turned.

Looking back, I still cringe and want to lie in the road and let the traffic run over me when I think how stupid I've been.

We exchanged emails, traded sweet nothings and promises. I was seduced — I wanted love. Only thing was, he wanted lust — he's a man, after all. But everything lined up. "Love is blind," they say. Well, I don't know if it was love or me. Blind and stupid.

I should have smelled a rat when he told me his two sons didn't speak to him, nor his ex-wife. In my defence, he seemed like the real deal. Educated, witty, intelligent, had degrees, was successful and solvent. Even the fuzzy little photo on the website couldn't hide the fact that he looked normal. He sounded normal too, when we spoke on the phone. But what can you really tell?

"You're the one, it's *beshert*, destiny," he told me, before we had even met. Did I mention that my head was turned?

> I tried not to feel too hurt as I headed for the fridge

Online it's easy to give yourself away, be anyone — very different from doing it in real time, face to face. After all, how many people have told me they knew someone who knew someone who had met someone and fallen in love online? Actually, not many, but I'm an eternal optimist.

So my CEO flew to London and I looked after him for a week. We laughed together and I liked him and felt good, and by the end of the week I told him I loved him. Maybe that's why I feel so betrayed. I knew something wasn't right — woman's intuition. Meanwhile, he met my mother, my friends, drank coffee in my local coffee shop, sampled North London life. Now my mother asks after him. He's waiting for me in America, I lie.

From safe back home in the States he emailed, explaining why I wasn't "the one" after all. It was the old story — a previous relationship he couldn't let go of. "In my head, we had three in the bed, you me and my ex-girlfriend," he confessed.

I tried to be furious with him, but women always blame themselves, first port of call. I tried not to feel too hurt as I headed for the fridge.

My learned daughter (all 19 years of her) pointed out: "How come if he was with you, he couldn't just be with you?" Indeed. Personally, I think we were four in the bed — me, him, the ex and a plastic box called Dell.

But nothing is straightforward. He wants to be friends and there was undeniably a connection between us. So we keep on emailing, polite, no flirting, which is hard for a serial flirt like me, although he bends the rules and says: "We *will* meet again, you're wonderful."

So, do I live in hope or lie in the road?

This is an occasional column. Elizabeth Green runs Trusting Love relationship courses (elizabeth@yestorelationships.co.uk)

Look, I'm a columnist for The Jewish Chronicle

My Best Production

23 YEARS LATER

CHAPTER 21

I am on a Landmark Education leadership course. We have weekend two coming up and I have the option to do it – in Bombay.

I have Mahesh's precious office number. I am going to call and let him know.

He's out of the office. It takes three calls, fear grows, will he remember me, will he want to remember me?

'It's Elizabeth, you used to know me as Veena, I'm coming to Bombay tomorrow can we meet?'

I say it without pausing for breath and it's silent on the line for a minute.

'My fatty bum bum.'

I blush.

'I'll give you my cell number, call me when you arrive.'

OMG yesssss!

I'm off to Bombay. I leave an upset husband, upset because he doesn't like me any more, upset because I'm leaving my kids behind, upset because I'm going to have more fun than him. Life for him was always a competition and he had to be the winner.

This time, I win.

I'm staying, by coincidence, with a friend of Mahesh's. Aruna is a film maker too.

Arriving in Bombay is like coming home: the heat, the noise and the people. The taxis are hooting and hooting as they weave through the traffic. I'm tense for a moment. My body has not remembered what to do, then I take a breath, sit back, and trust the universe, and of course the driver. The springs in the taxi are broken, it's not comfortable, not like our swish London cabs.

But in India nothing is broken or discarded.

Out of the dusty window, I see my favourite Bombay sight, a

moped carrying a whole family, mother, father and two kids.

I meet Aruna for the first time. She is wonderful. She leads Landmark courses so we talk and soul-search and invent 'possibilities', a cornerstone of the work. I'm my own person again, not stifled by a critical husband or demanding children, lovely but demanding children. At night, after our dinner we devour Alphonso mangoes. I score a mango as if to break it into quarters, then I peel back the skin, and just suck the delicious fruit down to the stone. Aruna does the same and the juice runs down our arms, we giggle and keep sucking.

I speak to Mahesh every day but he's too busy and I'm on the course. Today, the last day, Aruna and I are going to a march beside Juhu Beach, a protest march where all the movie people will be present. Movies are magic in India, everyone watches the movies and reveres the stars, and he's going to be there.

We have to drive for an hour and it's hot, oh so hot. Thankfully, we have a driver.

'What do I wear, Aruna, to greet a long-lost love I haven't seen for twenty three years?'

We laugh, she knows about my passion, and she's curious. How is this small, sensual English woman connected to one of their leading filmmakers?

'Aruna, will I recognise him?'

'Yes, look over there.'

The driver has let us out and she's pointing.

I'm nervous and then he sees me and comes over.

'Elizabeth, how are you? Come here let me hug you.'

Suddenly, that feeling is there all over again, never extinguished, even after so much time.

'You're the same,' he says.

'You too, a little fatter' I say, being a little daring.

'So what are you doing here?'

'I came with Aruna.'

'Here, let's walk.'

He takes my hand and my body remembers his body, I'm drawn to him, my heart and soul suddenly open to him. He moves in and out of the crowd, talking to people, not always by my side. But I feel safe and wanted, even when he's not beside me and, when he's close by my side, his presence makes my heart beat, his strong arm protects me.

The march stops and we get out of the strong sun, we sit in the chowki, the police compound. All the TV cameras turn towards him, they all want to interview him. I sit just out of shot.

When the attention on him stops, he says: 'Shall I take you out tonight, and paint the town red and take you home?'

'Who says I'll want to go home?'

'You're funny, I'll send my car.'

He sends his car a few hours later. The car sweeps through the Bombay night traffic. The windows are slightly darkened and I sit back and watch. At every traffic light, beggars swarm round the car, they realise it must be carrying someone important. But it's just me, feeling special and important for a moment.

He gets me out of the car and we go to dinner. He's so attentive, he loves that I'm wearing black.

'My mother always wore black, it makes me think of her.' I know he loved her so very much.

He holds my hand, his words are like food and drink, I barely eat anything.

'I'm going to drive back with you.'

In the car we sit as close as possible. He tells me how his life has been, his sadness about Parveen, his new guru, UG Krisnamurti. He had to choose between Parveen and UG. He chose UG.

'I feel so guilty.'

This makes me love him even more. Why are we all so in love with this guy?

He leans over and kisses me, it's like a spark of electricity going through my body. It's just a kiss, that's all we can share now, kisses and words.

I'm overwhelmed.

His phone rings, it's his brother, his brother who's drinking too much. 'Just tell him you love him,' I whisper.

'I love you,' he tells his brother. I love to contribute.

Thank God, the journey takes an hour so the deliciousness lasts a whole hour, which seems like a lifetime.

When we get to Aruna's house, he takes my hand and helps me out of the car.

'When I'm with you I want to cry,' he says. 'You do something to me. I feel so open and vulnerable with you.'

'Me too. Me too. I feel like crying.'

We hug very, very tightly, I'm wishing the moment would never end.

'Goodbye.'

'Goodbye my sweetheart,' he says 'I just really love you, I can't explain.'

We hug, tighter.

'Me too, goodbye.'

Aruna is waiting up for me inside.

A look at my face and she knows.

'You really love him don't you?'

'Yes.'

Next day, I leave my beloved Bombay and Mahesh for London; feels as if I can fly home without the plane. I have a few hours to compose myself, brush the glow from my eyes, get into housewife mode again.

A few weeks later it's the third weekend of the course and it's lunch break. We're sitting in the local Indian café in Camden Town rushing through our meal. My phone pings.

It's a text, and I don't know what to do, I've never texted before. I turn to my coursemate, Andrew

'Andrew, what do I do?'

I'm so excited, I'm hesitant, not sure what to say, time to harness my inner teenager.

The texting builds and builds. He's five hours ahead of me, so he waits impatiently for my day to start and then he's writing and writing. He follows me on my day, we laugh and joke and send sweet nothings. So intimate, those small words on a small screen.

One day I text him and tell him, 'I've never seen a movie of yours?'

'I will give you some titles. Watch my new movie.'

'What is it about? Tell me, because I won't understand a word.'

'It's sourced from my own sadness.'

Wow, is he really so anguished? My heart breaks, breaks a little more than it is already broken.

I want to ask what the anguish is? Is it from missing me? I skip the question.

I watch his movie. It's sad and melodramatic and very Indian. I'm not loving it, but I'm loving him. I tell him that and somehow he seems to start melting into the distance and slowly we're not so much in touch.

'Why do you work so much?' I ask him one day.

'To hide the pain,' he writes back.

He just wants to be loved, I wish it could have been me, I would have had your brown babies, been a good Indian wife.

We drift, he's filming, I'm mothering.

Then I decide I must make one more visit. I disguise it as a course, to my unsuspecting husband who, by now, is a little distant anyway and I let Mahesh know I'm coming.

Aruna welcomes me one more time. I love Bombay, that frisson of excitement and we're going to the Indian TV awards, Aruna and Mahesh are to be judges. So I'm going to see my sweetie.

I have bought myself a very fancy salwar kameez, that's baggy pants on a drawstring waist and a long tunic to go over it, and a long scarf to wear backwards with the ends floating down my back. Mine is turquoise kind of netting lined in plain turquoise fabric embroidered in gold, and I have long, dangling earrings intricate and Indian style. I'm feeling kind of special and nervous inside to see Mahesh.

The speakers tell jokes, they start in English and then tell the punchline in Hindi, and suddenly I'm surrounded by people laughing their heads off, whilst I have no idea of what is going on. I'm frustrated.

Aruna goes backstage and I'm sitting alone. Suddenly, a black clad Mahesh comes on to the stage, his presence almost shocks me, it's like a punch in the chest, I'm slightly gasping for breath.

Afterwards, I see him across the room.

'You're here, I'm just texting you,' he says.

He points across the room.

'My wife is here, I'll call you.'

I just nod and go to find Aruna for the long ride home.

'Did you tell Mahesh I was here?'

'I'm so sorry I didn't think of it.'

My last two days are spent texting and calling. We try to plan to meet but there's never any time.

My last day is nearly over, I'm anguished, is this going to happen? It is, we're pushing through.

He tells me: 'Take a cab to the hotel near the airport and I will meet you there at 5:30am.'

Yes 5:30 is the only time left to meet before my flight.

I hate to wake Aruna, but at 4:30am I shake her awake, I have to say goodbye and thank you and love you.

'Dearest Aruna thank you so much.'

'Take care.'

She may know we're meeting. I'm not going to tell her now, she's sleepy anyway.

I'm in the cab, Mahesh texts.

'Are you near?'

'Not sure, this is so strange, who needs the movies when we're meeting like this?'

'Indeed, life is stranger than art!' he tells me.

Ever the movie director, ever the artist, loves the drama my sweetie. Outside the hotel, his car draws up and the doorman is watching with interest, he's recognised Mahesh. I'm looking only at Mahesh.

The doorman tries to take my bag, but Mahesh takes it and his driver puts it into the boot of the car.

'I'm not going to drop you at the airport, I hate goodbyes.'

I get in and sit as close as possible. He holds my hand and hugs me, there's nothing much to say at this early hour.

Now we're pulling up at the airport, yes in spite of what he said, it's the airport and it's time for goodbye.

I'm so sad and happy at the same time. Half an hour later my phone rings.

'Are you intoxicated?' he asks me

'Yes' and I know what he means.

I fly radiantly back to London.

This is our last meeting, last moment of love.

MÉNAGE A TROIS

CHAPTER 22

I left India as Ma Deva Veena, divine musical instrument of the master. I had worn orange for two years, stretched the brief a little to purple and mustard yellow as designed by Ma Prem Vasudha, seamstress, Italian cook and great friend and confidante.

My mother was at the airport, disapproving but ready to meet me. She looked older, much older and still cross.

She still had the big house in Hampstead Garden Suburb, but no room for me she said, that was upsetting. After a couple of nights I found friends, strangers, and eventually Janine in Willesden, who had done the Est Landmark training course. I moved in with my mostly orange clothes.

Seems Est was best in the West, Bhagwan in the East.

But I wasn't well. I took a bus to Selfridges, but the amount of people scared me. I fled home again. I had a terrible rash on my arms, and some spots on my face, legs and other parts.

A friend introduced me to Alice, an astronomer who wanted me to detox and eat only grapes, pounds and pounds of grapes, for a few weeks. I was fabulous on grapes, so much sugar, so much happiness. After all, sugar is my drug of choice. Some people are addicted to cocaine, sugar is my cocaine.

But the rash got worse, and eventually Alice sent me to see Dr. Sharma. This was my introduction to homeopathic medicine, a momentous introduction it turns out. It worked then, still works for me now.

But I still feel so unloved and unwanted. In India you could sit at the feet of the guru, and ask him questions, burning questions about life, whilst looking into his eyes, warm pools of acceptance and love, no judgment, just acceptance.

At least that's what I tell people when they ask.

'Is he real? How did you know?'

I told the guru I always seemed to fall in love with people who were not available, and that I would like to fall in love with someone and have them fall in love with me. But I was always attracted to people I couldn't have.

Bhagwan said that unconsciously I did not really want to fall in love, so that is why I chose people with whom my love could never be fulfilled. He told me I chose them not for themselves but for their inaccessibility, and that if they became available, I would drop the idea of pursuing them.

I told him I either tried to keep people away or would just go and grab, neither of which worked very well.

But did I listen? Did I do what he said?

I remember when I was 17 or so, still living at home. My mother told me: 'Just remember, no-one is good enough for you.' I was put in my place. Then, too late, she added 'But you are better than everyone!'

Not sure if that was before or after she took me to the psychologist. When she was out of the room he explained, 'She is never going to change, it's you that has to.'

Sure made meeting 'the one' difficult. It was funny, there must have been a point when I trusted her. One summer, when I was 15, my mother sent me away to Jewish camp, and I made some new friends who came round on Sunday afternoons for tea. I heard only people who felt comfortable with their parents invited friends round to the family home. I liked having people round to my house. Made me feel important. Was I trying to prove something?

My mother, I believe, took it as trust. Ricky and I used to sit upstairs in my bedroom and mess about. Yes, I had discovered sex and around that time I 'did the deed.'

But with Paul.

On our sitting room couch with the silk-covered cushions.

While Tony Bennett played.

He introduced me to Tony Bennett who sang, 'I Left My Heart in San Francisco' so hauntingly.

I remember it as the song I was deflowered to!

Romantic.

Bella and I went together on Sunday nights to the Jewish youth club at the St. John's Wood Liberal synagogue, my father used to come and pick me up and drive me home. I was on the synagogue committee helping arrange charity dances.

Team player was hard for me. With no sense of self, it was hard to be in the pack and feel I had something to contribute.

I spent my whole life looking for approval, specially from my mother. That's why I married so late, couldn't find anyone who wanted me, and then I only married David because he asked me.

I wasn't 'in love' with him, but I sure wanted to be married. Yes, I remember, on the day I got married breathing out and thinking to myself, 'Yay, I got married, I'm home and dry.'

Oh little did I know. But for me, at first, it was novel that someone wanted me, wanted me around. He loved my sassiness, my directness, my sense of humour. He'd never met anyone like me before.

He had a flat in Catford, South East London, when I met him. He'd got himself on the property ladder so I moved in. I was a North London girl so his humble South East London abode was like a foreign country.

One Sunday, while we were out, he got his parents to come round and help redecorate. We came home to find they had left much mess and debris behind.

'Who left those cigarette butts on the window sill?'

'Oh, that was Tom.'

'Who's Tom?'

'Tom's the lodger.'

'What do you mean the lodger?'

'It's a long conversation.'

'Ok try me.'

'Well, my mother lives with two men. One is Ernie, her husband, the other one is Tom, but Tom is my dad.'

Bombshell.

'What do you mean?'

I had not yet met my now ex-husband's parents, all three of them. My ex-husband was brought up by them all, thinking everyone had two dads. Delusional? Eventually, I think at school he realised this wasn't normal. He never asked questions, after all he's a guy. But when I met him, and he told me about them, I shrieked, in shock, in disbelief.

Then my questions started.

'Do you talk about it? Have you asked them about it? What is going on?'

He told me the story. I could not believe he had never sat down with them to talk about it. He had not. That is until I heard about it.

Seems Betty and Tom had been girlfriend and boyfriend. Tom went off to war, joined the RAF, and by the time he came back, she had met Ernest and married him. Poor Tom had nowhere to go but he had a very handy pension, so he went to stay with them for a short while and never left.

I always felt so bad for Ernie, his whole married life was a threesome, a 'ménage a trois', very risqué in their day, from their background, their working class background. Tom's pension bought them a house, something Betty and Ernie would have never been able to afford, and gave them some security so they all stayed together, and then children came: Stephen was born, then Robert ... and then David.

Put them in a room together and you would be approaching Tom, hand extended, saying 'Hello Mr. Neville, you must be David's dad.' He was, but he was Tom Yorke!

Yes, indeed he was, unmistakably the father. If only he had left after fathering his illegitimate son, no-one would have ever known.

By the time I met and married David they had all three been together for 30 years. No one went anywhere without the other two.

Ernie was the only one who would speak about it. Seems he was very aggrieved to share his wife. You see, the sleeping arrangements were very novel. Betty had the double room and the boys, well men, Tom and Ernie, each had a single room.

We had a theory. We reckoned they took turns. Monday, Wednesday and Friday were Ernie's nights, Tuesday, Thursday and Saturday were Tom's nights. Even David reluctantly laughed about it.

He called them his real dad 'Tom' and his pretend dad 'Ernie'.

Sue, wife of eldest son Stephen, told us Ernie had a 'fancy woman' as working class people referred to a lover. She knew because she used to drive him to his assignations. I don't think, from what he later told us, his heart was in it, I think it was just a form of revenge.

But Betty was strong and strident and ruled them both with a rod of iron.

'Tom is more helpful around the house. Ernie is a better gardener.' Sounds like an arrangement we should all consider.

But I was outraged and tried to encourage David and our kids to address Tom as respectively, 'Dad and Grandad.' I wasn't outraged at their behaviour, I was outraged at the lack of truth, level of deceit, when all was there to see.

David did take Tom out for lunch and have a heart to heart. Betty never broke ranks.

They didn't like me because I wanted it all out in the open, the truth to be told, because, here's the rub:

David's mother lied to him about who his real father was, and if you can't trust your mother, your primary care-giver, your first ever significant relationship, who can you trust? No, not a rhetorical question, she gave birth to you, she's your nearest and dearest, mummy dearest.

I think this coloured his whole world. But at least during my time, Tom got to be given his rightful role as 'Dad and Grandad.'

The three of them kept rather a private kind of life. They only came to see us about three times a year. They did come to Simon's bar mitzvah, heads held high and everyone treated them respectfully, even if they wondered quietly to themselves who David's doppelganger Tom was!

One Sunday afternoon they visited us in our suburban East Finchley home. It was a beautiful sunny day and we all ate lunch in the garden. As we finished lunch Betty requested David to grab a chair and take it down to the very far end of the garden.

So he did, and it was there they had a heart to heart.

'David,' Betty said, 'do you mind that I had a husband and a lover?'

I don't think I could have kept a straight face, but at least she finally admitted her situation, admitted it just that once. I guess mortality was beckoning and she wanted to set the record straight.

I tried to bond with my in-laws, tried valiantly. It was hard.

They moved out of London, to live near Stephen and Sue, and the grandchildren, I guess they felt closer to those grandchildren. Very occasionally us newlyweds would stay the night at their house.

I woke up one morning and my pyjamas smelled strange. I smelled as if I had spent the night in the pub, and was just waking up. It was still the days of smoke and smoking so if I HAD spent the night in a pub I would have smelled just like that.

But I was at home in bed.

They all three smoked, in the house, outside the house, the smell was everywhere. I think they had washed the sheets and hung them up to dry, and then smoked in the same room.

I nicknamed their house 'The Ashtray', any other comments I'm keeping to myself.

Then Betty died of lung cancer. I remember rushing up to their village near Milton Keynes one Sunday morning to see her body in the bed. The boys, Tom and Ernie, were devastated, Ernie was not happy.

He had hoped Tom would die first so he could have some quality time with Betty, and now here he was living with Tom, what a blow. This was not in his bloody plan.

Ernie, God bless him, died on his 'son' David's birthday, his 50th. We had a big party planned in a huge marquee in our back garden, carefully erected around all the beautiful plants that Nili and Andy had only just planted. Rosie was there with her much older Indian boyfriend, he played tablas and she danced, dressed in beautiful Indian robes. It was too late to cancel, so we held it as a joint celebration for David's birthday, and Ernie's passing.

Princess Diana died on David's birthday in 1997, so many deaths, so many birthdays. That day it was a luncheon party with my attention, at least, on the tragedy unfolding in the background on TV.

My return as Veena from India had not been easy, I was suffering from culture shock, I was like a displaced person and Janine and her flatmates moved at a fast pace, too fast for me.

My rash was worse since the grapes. Thank God, I was introduced to Dr. Sharma. Usually, his assistant took a case history with new patients, but after one look at me he took me straight upstairs to his consulting room and gave me a note. The note said: 'Three pears a day and bottled water only.' The only bottled water in the supermarket was Vichy, salty and fizzy. Not nice!

He sent me home, bandaged up, to rest and see him soon. I had little white pillules, homeopathic pills. Now I only take homeopathic pills, and vitamins, as needed. People come to my house needing aspirin and headache pills, but I never, ever keep them. I don't drink coffee and seldom eat red meat.

But I'm addicted to sugar. Dr. Sharma and I tried hard to beat it. Sometimes we did, sometimes we didn't.

Having such a terrible rash was an instant cure, food seemed unimportant, and uninviting. There were other times, the 'Getting divorced diet' worked well, or a special event in the future would give me inspiration. Sometimes I got happy enough to forget about food. Sometimes I was so sad all I wanted to do was eat myself into a stupor. A carb stupor would put me to sleep. Wonderful! Or so I thought at that time.

Two weeks later I was back, sitting in the Dr.'s waiting room, bandaged up. I thought I was a sight for sore eyes. But not for the tall distinguished looking gentleman who, looking concerned, leaned over and asked me 'Hi, are you OK, it looks painful.'

'It is, but Dr. Sharma's helping me.'

'That's good, do you need anything?'

He had a gruff distinguished voice, which fitted when I found out he was an actor and an MP. I love wonderful voices, and his was. He seemed to like me and wanted to help. I was too tired and sick to wonder, wonder what he was up to, what he wanted. Wasn't that all that men did? Want something?

He followed me out down the street.

'Hey beautiful lady, here's my number, please call me if you need someone to talk to. Do you have a number?'

I scribbled the number at Janine's and gave it to him.

A few days later he called me … from the House of Commons. Wasn't he supposed to be running the country? Was there not enough for him to do? Politics wasn't keeping him busy enough?

The rash went, it wasn't impetigo, it was scabies, infectious and scarring. But I was lucky; a couple of marks on my face faded away and there were no marks on my body from the gift I brought myself back from India.

Grateful and glamorous again, no, not totally, but it sounds good. Dr. Sharma offered me a job and somewhere to live. I moved into Seymour Place where the lines between working and off duty were a little blurred. Sharma owned 101 and 99 Seymour Place, and had made them adjoining. I lived at the top of 101 he lived in 99 and was quick to cross to my house when he needed a task doing, often.

Day I moved in, he finally prescribed for me, homeopathic injections. I had the 'becoming a new patient interview' done by Rowena, his much younger English girlfriend who also worked for him. He kept everyone close. He played guru, a little tubby Indian man sitting in his consulting room on his low chair. Some of his middle class women patients were taken in, I'd been with a real guru. I wasn't so impressed.

'I'm depressed,' I gushed to Rowena, 'so depressed.'

But the doctor had other notions and gave me injections to calm my hysteria and, to be honest, it all made sense. I injected myself each day, scary but it wasn't into a vein. Day Four, I forgot, and the hysteria rose, and rose, until I remembered,

'Oh my God, I forgot to inject.'

In a panic I ran to the dispensary to get what was needed. In that moment I realised it was not depression, it was indeed hysteria.

This is my go-to remedy, Ignatia. My calm me down, my even me out remedy.

I know there's a ground swell out there that says homeopathy doesn't work. The remedies, as they are known, were very effective for me, and the kids took them as well. If they didn't get 'pills' they cried. So they got them.

In fact I don't keep any medicines in my house, no need. When I looked after the kids they took nothing except antibiotics once each, growing up under my watchful eye.

Now they're grown up they do what they want, but all those years of not taking anything built up their immunities. I breast-fed everyone for a year. That built up their immunities too.

I loved breastfeeding. It hurt at first, hard little gums chomping on you, but it was so natural. Pregnancy agreed with me, my hormones rearranged themselves, I was sane, I was well, I bloomed. I watched what I ate, I didn't eat for two, I didn't need to, I didn't feel like it.

I never had morning sickness in my pregnancies. On our first trip abroad with the kids we took the cross-channel ferry from Plymouth to Roscoff, France. The sea was so rough I started throwing up almost from the minute we left shore. The waves were so high, pretty much everyone on board was sick and the crossing was a long six hours. Strangely, lying down in a bed near the bottom of the boat was the only thing that made me feel better. I felt very lucky. If that was anything like morning sickness, I missed nothing.

Having babies was my defining moment, my best production, the thing I was probably here on earth to do. Seems I was good at something, probably borne out of my own experiences growing up.

But it was easy, I just loved them, and knew what it felt like to be them most of the time. I spoke to them as equals, I was as strict as I could be. I told them when I was fed up, when I was tired, and when it was all too much for me to deal with.

Simon, my first born thank God, at 10 weeks old invented his own bedtime. After the third night in a row of going to sleep at 8, we decided 8 o'clock it was. But he was a little bugger, he liked the boob, wasn't ready to give that up in a rush. He's a boy after all! So at 8 months old he's still waking up at 2am for a feed.

Everyone, of course, compared notes, all the time. I had joined The National Childbirth Trust to meet women who had just given birth, and I had a group of women I met once a week, six of us, with six, oh-so-different babies, who all developed at their own rate, their own perfect rate. They were all perfect, the ones who wouldn't eat their food, the ones who woke up in the night for a quick extra feed. The tantrum throwers, the screamers, the projectile vomiters, it was all OK, every bit of it.

Simon wanted his 2am feed. So his dad David took over, offering water. Simon was outraged and let us know it. He screamed for 45 minutes the first night, 30 the next, just a few the next, and finally, he didn't wake up. I wore polo necks the whole time, tried not to hold him too near at bedtime so he wouldn't smell the milk. After all, to him, I was just a milk machine.

But the glory of kids was still in the distance.

The bandages put on by Dr. Sharma came off after a couple of weeks, no scarring, just a wounded ego. My ego that ran the show, that guided me, oh so wrong, that gave me false pride, killed hope, made me jealous and let me suffer when I couldn't be as good as other people, which was always.

I kept trying chocolate to make me feel better, which it did … for a mere moment. But it just put me back in the battle to keep weight off. My acupuncturist in London told me, 'Overeating is a fear of not being noticed in the world.' That sure rang a bell for me.

The guru in India had told me if I wanted to kill myself, he would help me find a better, quicker way than eating myself to death.

But plump or not, Andrew Faulds, my MP, seemed keen and interested, me too. It was time to test this out.

One beautiful sunny morning before work I took a walk along Seymour Place. I wore orange, the colour I had worn in India, not a robe but a long dress, and no knickers.

Andrew had a place in town nearby. So I walked up to his front door and rang his bell. I took a chance as his wife might be there, although I knew most of the time she stayed in the country. She was a diminutive woman I'd seen at Dr. Sharma's surgery.

I rang the bell, and he answered. He seemed a little surprised but quickly said 'My wife is in town.'

I was pretty sure she wasn't but that was my best offer and he turned me down.

IF YOU WANT TO DIE
I'LL GIVE YOU
A BETTER WAY

CHAPTER 23

I have a list of the music I played in India. I'm reading it, it contains many music icons. This was my introduction to some of them, an introduction that would last forever.

Joni Mitchell - 'Blue,' still playing her today.

Santana – 'Caravanserai', have the CD.

Dory Previn – 'Mythical Kings and Iguanas.' I remember these sad and poignant songs.

One day when I went into the frame shop on nearby Broadway they were playing Adele, a moody track. The storekeeper told me, 'I like listening to upset women sing.'

A sensitive Turkish man, sensitive to women and feelings, I'm thrilled.

Rod Stewart – 'Sing it again Rod.' Now Rod Stewart I know already. Barry, a teacher at John Kelly Boys school, introduced me to 'Maggie May,' a seminal song of Rod's. Heavenly. And then Rod Stewart was the cabaret at my brother's 50th birthday party. The first extravaganza he threw.

'Poo,' said my ex, such a purist, 'Rod Stewart, that's for women.'

Rod sang on toga night. There we all were, the guests, the waiters, the security men, all dressed in togas, such a leveler. I think Rod was the only one not wearing a toga. I loved him, all the women did, and some of the men. I was down the front waving my arms from side to side, above my head, as he sang 'Sailing'. I glance to my left, and there is my ex, well no, not waving his arms with quite my same rapt expression, but, watching and listening intently.

'So you liked his performance?'

I'm amused.

'He was very good.'

Bob Marley – 'Natty Dread.' I knew about Bob Marley too from the people I met at Quaesitor the growth centre in Willesden. I think I slept to a few of his tracks whilst doing therapy with Simon Meyerson, yes, his was a unique method of therapy.

What caught my eye was Flute from the Andes, 'Concerto de Aranjuez,' I loved this music and I haven't played it for so long. As I walked through Times Square 42nd street subway station one day, this was the music I heard. Must buy some, play some. If I close my eyes I will remember India.

I have lists of meditation times, vitamins I took. What I ate for lunch, how much I spent on rickshaws and how much a popai cost. Was I methodical or just had too much time on my hands?

If I close my eyes and squint, could I have written the list last week? But I was busy in India. I worked, I cleaned the bathrooms and toilets in all the rooms in the ashram, the rooms of most of the high-up disciples, although never in the inner sanctum where Bhagwan the master and his closest people lived.

After a few months of that, I was sent to the kitchen, a promotion? Not sure. Deeksha, the large Italian woman in charge, yelled and screamed most of the day.

After all, the guru said: 'Be in the market place, not of the market place.' Then he sent Deeksha for me to practice on. It was hard, but then enlightenment, climbing to the top of the mountain, was not promised to be easy. Might just as well cook food, wash dishes, after all, everything was enlightenment - work, everything, even now.

Andrew McCarthy, a successful actor, director and now writer, summed it up so well when I asked him a question at a talk he was giving. 'Is anything possible? Is that what you are saying?' I ask him.

His eyes narrow as if he's looking inwards.

'I get bored quickly (laughter). Life is long in certain ways and you've got to have something to do during the day.'

I'm thinking, that's just what I say, doesn't matter what you do, we're all just 'doing' something, getting through the day!

'You've got to do something that makes you feel. The first time I acted, I went, Oh, there I am. First time I wrote about travel, Oh there I am. The first time I directed I thought, Oh, there I am. Writing this book…'

He's about to launch his first novel, Just Fly Home.

'I found Lucy's voice, I thought, Oh there I am. All the things I do for a living are creative. I have absolutely no skill, no applicable skill to do anything. I just follow the things that make me feel like me in a certain way.'

Then he dropped the bomb.

'Biggest gift I've had is I never wanted to be anybody else just me, or a better version of me.'

Hear hear, anybody seen me? Send her back.

India, this was my big step, a new continent and I'm on my own kid! Looking back, was it like going to America? I chose carefully once again, no language problem here, and a bonus, in India I will be able to cross the road without killing myself. Countries which had been under British rule still drive on the left side like England.

'I want my mother,' Soma the child I'm accompanying, is screaming in the airport.

'It'll be OK,' I whisper, trying to comfort her.

But as you know, we got there and she was dispatched to her father.

We will remember London as a far away distant rainy place, grey and sometimes unfriendly and wish for its cooling climate. But then we will be glorying in the bright sunshine, which makes all the colours look bright and luminous. The women wear saris and salwar kameez, pants under a tunic, to you and me. I wore the beautiful turquoise one with the netting, embellished in gold for my son's bar mitzvah, to cover me up, belly and all.

They wear bright jewel colours and even poor people smile and are bright, and when they hear my English accent in public they crowd round and ask questions.

I'm on a train one day going to Goa to meet my cute Canadian boyfriend and eat hash cookies while celebrating the full moon. They crowd round.

'My cousin lives in Manchester. Do you know my cousin?' As if?

'You are wearing toe rings, are you married?' (Married women wear toe rings in their culture.)

They were kind and curious, and questioning.

Once again, I'm on my life's quest, to find someone to love, and more poignantly, someone to love me. More than love me, someone who can't live without me. I'm away from my family with new beginnings, no past, and right now, not much future.

Only problem, when I get there, who is there? Me! Many nice Jewish girls from North London had escaped to sit at the feet of the guru and ask esoteric questions. Or were they? It's a place where anything is allowed, if only you give yourself permission.

I have never worn orange, now I'm about to, all the time, and no-one will care if it suits me or not. I'm on my own here. A week later, I'm taken off to the tailor.

I don't know where the darts should go, I never had anything made, I just buy clothes in a shop, someone else moulded them to my imagined shape.

But I look OK. I'm making it up as I go along. But the results are surprisingly good, and I look the part as I put my mala back over my head. Everyone is wearing the same long string of brown beads with a picture of Osho Rajneesh hanging at the bottom. There will become a time when I will feel naked without it around my neck, we're not there yet.

So, it's early days at the ashram and, armed with a new name, new clothes and a new outlook, I'm ready to go to Darshan; private meeting, there will be maybe 20 of us around him, sitting near his feet. When it is my turn I will go forward, sit close, and ask him a question.

I like new, scary and new. London, Poona or New York, is there a difference? Same struggle, different location.

I have a burning question - does it burn more since I arrived in Poona? I move forward to sit at his feet and ask my important question.

'Bhagwan, I'm not sure if I want to live or die?'

The other people sitting around saw his eyes twinkle, as he gently played with me. I was deeply unaware but I heard his answer.

'If you want to die, I will give you a better way than eating yourself to death.'

I gasp, and protest.

'Of course I want to live' thinking to myself 'Do I?'

'No, you will not tell me now, you will choose if you want to live or die and come back tomorrow and tell me.'

I ponder the whole night to find an answer, but look, I'm still alive, seems I found an answer.

Next night I said to the guru: 'I don't think what I've been doing is living, can you help me to really live?'

But then I'm off down the road to the local café to eat cake and curd and Indian sweets.

Eating is the Indian national pastime. New York is a foodie capital, and London is full of sweets and chocolate, great Swiss chocolate! So wherever I go, food is there until I discover the food is not the problem.

The problem is how much I hate myself. I don't want to be that fat person on the Tube scoffing chocolate covering it with my hand. Don't know who I'm hiding from, no-one else cares, even though secretly I'm hoping they do.

I use food as anaesthetic, soothing balm, and anger management. It doesn't work, I know that, but I still walk round the supermarket hiding sugary snacks underneath the fruit for secret snacks later.

Then I had an epiphany, a moment, when I started loving myself, and I decided I was good enough. All that time I'd been looking for someone to love, and there I was all the time, me, that wit, that comedienne, that intellectual, that sexy creature.

So I forgave myself for over-eating and beating myself up and always judging myself, for not being a good enough daughter, sister, mother, parent, friend, wife, human being, for loving chocolate more than life.

Here in New York, I think of that moment, often. The mission – to love myself, which in turn will make me loveable.

Living alone in New York I have a wholesome refrigerator! I'm snack-free here, well mostly! Of course I have 20 menus in the drawer for ordering in and Westside Market two blocks away is open twenty four hours out of twenty four. But I've only walked up the road twice in the middle of the night to buy emergency ice cream or grab chocolate. Cross my heart and hope to die.

No really, it doesn't taste nice any more. I hate chocolate cake and chocolate ice cream and all things chocolate except chocolate itself.

I'm the calm before the storm. I'm the woman who's cleared the sugar out of her brain. I'm not addicted any more, for now.

I played in India, some of it was beautiful, some painful. I loved, and lost, and loved again. But he's another story, he still has a little piece of my heart as I'm humming Lara's Theme.

FAMILY SECRETS AND BREAKDOWNS

CHAPTER 24

New York New York, so great they named it twice.

But it's my third continent.

Pretty good, I hear many of you say. Do you know what it's like moving to another country, even one that speaks the same language as you? Or so they say!

After 1982, it was a long time until I came back.

Post-divorce it seemed to have a magnetic pull on me, and in fact some of my ancestors did settle in the USA. Turns out my grandfather was scheduled to be one of them but he got sick, according to Cousin Robert, and got off the boat in England. Probably not even quite knowing where he was, with a new name. When immigrants arrived at the turn of the last century, names were changed at the border. Foreign sounding names disappeared.

My grandfather, Ephraim, my mother's father came from Russia, but for sure his name in Russia was unlikely to have been Bull. My father's family, from Poland, the Greens, had probably also been given that name at the border. I found out recently his name was changed from Terkeltaub. I could have been Elizabeth Terkeltaub, doesn't have quite the same ring.

My mother had two brothers, Harold and Monty, and a sister Annette. Montague, Monty to all, moved to Toronto many years ago, we never visited, Robert did. When he got sick, my mother was so reluctant to go she was sitting in the plane, on the tarmac at Heathrow, when news came through he had just died. Never mind, she got there in time for the burial. I don't think she was too bothered, she didn't do family my mother.

She didn't do people, preferred men to women, and business to her kids and motherhood. I had a 'big' birthday and invited 20 women to my party and only two males, my sons. Elaine who had worked for my mother from the age of 15 begged me to invite her, but I didn't.

The party was wonderful, we went round the group, each person took a turn to speak and told a story about our relatedness, how they knew me, how long and spilled a few secrets about themselves too.

Next day Elaine phoned my mother: 'Alma, you should have been there, it was a wonderful party.'

'Who was there?'

'All women.'

'Boring!' my mother retorted.

So it was even more shocking when I found out she had considered adopting Robert. Cousin Louie had told me this, one afternoon while we drank tea.

Robert was Annette's secret son, adopted by Harold and his wife Claire. Virtually no one knew, not even Robert. I didn't know. Annette lived in New York. I remember when I was very small seeing her off on one of the big liners crossing the ocean, she made trips to England, came to birthday parties, we called her Auntie Netty, Robert did too. Then, aged 14, he found a birth certificate in a drawer at his parents' house, which told him Netty was his mother.

He saved this earth-shattering news, kept it to himself, internalised his feelings. Stayed quiet, kept schtum (Yiddish) saved it up for a nervous breakdown later in life. True, Harold and Claire said nothing either. In those days it was all about 'sparing the child.' Spare turned to despair!

Men, why do they do that? As soon as I heard, I wanted to know everything. As soon as the words were out of Louie's mouth, I rushed to ask my mother what had happened.

My mother and I never spoke about personal stuff, she didn't ask and I didn't speak usually. Now shockingly she told me she and my father had considered adopting Robert, but had realised there was only six months between him and Philip, so everyone would know he was adopted. So it was decided Harold and Claire would adopt him.

Next stop was the hospital where Uncle Harold was getting cancer treatment, his cancer was advancing fast. There was not much time and this was a big secret which needed discussing before he died. Everybody in Robert's life was related, just not quite in the way we all knew. He was Robert's uncle. Grandpa was Grandpa, my mother was Auntie Alma. Everything was almost alright with the world. Except the lie that had sat with Robert and Harold and Claire.

Families, whose grief do they think they save by keeping everything secret? Whose feelings are hurt, whose reputation damaged?

When eventually the truth comes out, as it usually does, then the hurt begins.

Harold was pleased to see me, and not surprised by my news, it was almost as if he'd been waiting for someone to say something, as long as it wasn't him.

'Please can you talk about it to Robert? Robert knows about Netty, his mother, but he won't talk about it. Please see if you can get him to talk?'

God, I get all the good jobs. Robert could be very aggressive, always right, shouting at me, everyone, angry and usually taking it out on his wife April.

Robert married later in life, and he became an older father. Yes, I know, sometimes older parents are more patient, not Robert.

He adamantly refused to talk about it with me.

'None of your business.'

'Your dad wanted me to talk with you, I only just found out.'

'I'm fine,' he was almost snarling.

'OK.'

He was not OK but I was not prepared to argue.

Many years later I sat in Cherry Tree Woods near my house in East Finchley, while he sobbed and remonstrated and cursed and beat himself up.

'I feel hopeless, I'm having a breakdown, can't concentrate, do anything, look after myself any more. Let me stay for a couple of days?'

He did. I hate myself for saying this, but I think this was the only time I liked Robert, Robert humble, a little lost, not so full of himself was a nice sight for the eyes.

Only problem, we were all due to go on holiday with him and his family plus another couple, and although April was mad at him most days, she stayed behind to take over looking after him, while I went ahead with Georgia, his daughter Laura and the other couple.

Robert told me much later, 'I wouldn't have gone on holiday with them.'

Now you tell me, and yes they were difficult, aggressive people, a Nigerian woman and her bald Jewish husband, with his failed business, and dying ego. Thank God she wore the trousers.

They had brought their daughter with them, a friend for Laura. Laura's father, also called Robert, let's call him Robert P., spoke to his daughter in the third person. A pet hate, oh my God, I could barely listen. Georgia watched me seething, she nearly had to physically restrain me. I might not have been good at many things, or anything according to my mother, but kids, I just spoke to them the way I would speak to anyone, young or old. Just as myself, no mystery there. This guy was terrible.

'Darling, daddy wants to make sure you're not hungry any more. Daddy wants to know you're alright.'

Poor kid, let's hope she had a chance at growing up normal. I know by aged 10 my kids told me what they thought about almost everything. They didn't suffer fools gladly. 'Judge Jacob' (see TV show 'Trust Me I'm a Teenager') aged 13 spoke up.

We were in Egypt, in Hurghada on the Red Sea. But the fancy holiday spot was Sharm el Sheikh and we were not there. April had bought an apartment in Hurghada, we stayed in the next door apartment.

Everything in Hurghada was half finished. I called it 'half built Hurghada'. Our apartment was owned by an upright Englishman, her friend Ian, but the apartment also was half finished! No curtains, piles of rubble everywhere. Inside each room, it looked as if work was started, and never finished. The cooker didn't work, the AC worked intermittently and we were paying for this. Bloody cheek! The road up to the apartments consisted of sand dunes, which you had to climb every day, and the sun was only over the pool half the day as the pool was enclosed on three sides by the apartment building.

So there we were with Robert P. and his wife, in half-built Hurghada, while cousin Robert was having his nervous breakdown in London.

When I first told Georgia I had booked to go on holiday with April and Robert she was dumbfounded.

'Are you crazy? Are you feeling alright?'

I defended very half-heartedly, knowing she was right.

After a couple of days playing catch the sun round the pool we all decided to take a trip to historic Cairo, to stay with Ian. For this we caught a bus from El Gouna bus station, a hot and uncomfortable six-hour journey.

Mind you, what a thrill to see the River Nile, even though I'm partisan, Jewish you know. But this is biblical, historical. This river has been there thousands of years. We have history, the Six Day War, and then there's a bridge named after the one battle the Egyptians won. One battle in a war they lost, and a whole bridge named '6th October Bridge'.

We were up early to go to the Cairo Museum to see Tutankhamun's gold sarcophagus and many other statues and coffins and jewels. I had seen this amazing collection in London, the others had not.

It was a crowded spectacle, the Egyptians were not to everyone's taste. The men fitted every stereotype in the book and I had beautiful Georgia with me so we elicited much attention. Ian's driver lent for the day, had, in the same breath shown us pictures of his kids and declared undying love for Georgia.

'Please Georgia,' he asked in his broken English, 'please come and meet me later.'

There was nothing I needed to guide her on, she's sensible and her head is not easily turned. She must be my changeling daughter, she's nothing like me. Me, whose head is turned in a second, she's almost too far the other way, and she's a bloody good pretender. From aged eight onwards, she didn't show you how she was feeling. But she jumped on me, and corrected me if I got too emotional. We had spent enjoyable holidays together, usually just the two of us. This was more stressful, always is when the pack has to make decisions. This was worse with such unreasonable people whom we barely knew.

As we left the museum I decided to run into the gift shop to buy some postcards. I kept everybody waiting. Of course I didn't know how difficult it was for the driver to stop. I was sorry and sweating as I rushed back to the car, and as I jumped in, Robert P. let loose, abusive, in front of all the kids, incoherent with rage, accusatory and aggressive. In fact, he was just plain NASTY.

We drove back to Ian's in silence, we had settled into camps, me and Georgia against the others.

That night, at dusk, we went on the Nile and had a feast on Ian's boat. It was Ramadan and the Egyptians broke the fast nightly. We were on the boat as the light went down, and the sun set. It was magical and the others faded into the night as we reveled in the history and magnificence of the place.

It couldn't have been further away from our lives in London, and Ian and his servants were lovely, everyone except Robert P. was agreeable and welcoming.

Robert P. was not forgiving either.

By the time we returned to Hurghada three days later, April and Robert and their son Mark had arrived and Georgia and I were ready to leave the unpleasantness. But our ticket homeward bound was a few days away.

Ian rescued us and booked us into the Sheraton Hotel on the Red Sea, at a reduced rate, and April got us a car and a driver, trying to make a nice gesture I suppose. But April was such a disorganised person that the car went first to the hotel, thinking it was picking us up there. Three hours went by, the sun beat down while we were wasting the glorious day standing beside our suitcases in the apartment lobby waiting and waiting for a car, that eventually after its unwarranted journey, showed up to take us back to the hotel.

April had insisted on coming with us in the car, to make sure we were fine, and get herself dropped off at the beach. Now as if we hadn't been delayed long enough, first we had to find a cash dispenser. Finally, thank God, she got out with a wave and said goodbye.

Now the Sheraton on the Red Sea was an hour outside Hurghada and there we were, stuck in splendor. No sympathy for sure, it was us and all the Italians and too much food.

So with nowhere to go and nothing to do, we ate, and sunbathed and swam in the balmy waters and ate some more! One day, April came over with everyone to sit on the beach at the Sheraton. They didn't sit with us, but she came over to see if we were OK. Was she looking a little sheepish, or did I imagine it?

Next time we saw them was at the airport.

In the cab home, April even managed to remind me I owed her money for Mark's bar mitzvah gift. Had to pay up! By the time I reached our house I felt well and truly stung in every sense of the word.

This wasn't my first trip to Egypt. I had seen the pyramids and the Sphinx and shopped in the Soukh the first time. But now, this was the last time, my last trip to Egypt.

New York was certainly more my cup of tea. I came here for 10 days as a gift to myself, stayed alone and explored. My surroundings and my psyche! Both were certainly interesting.

That was when I discovered the Tribeca Grand for the first time.

And of course I was always on the look-out for a date!

GEORGIA ON MY MIND

CHAPTER 25

The word 'No.'

The hardest word, was I told it when I was a baby? For sure, I've been a parent, I've used it. Until I read the enlightenment books and then started saying:

'Oh look at this, why don't you come over here and look at this,' known as a distraction technique.

But my kids were quite well behaved, did not throw public tantrums, throw themselves on the ground. They were not shy, they spoke to people.

Much later they did commercials. Aged two Georgia did a nappy commercial. I wasn't even inside the studio while she worked. When I saw it afterwards, I was astonished.

'How did they get her to do that?' she was bending down looking through her legs.

When she went for an interview at the fancy girls private school I was planning to send her to, it wasn't a problem. Georgia was expected at age four and a half to go in and see the headmistress, without me accompanying her.

Some were in floods of hysterical tears, clinging wildly to mum, and dad. Mine, I whispered in her ear, 'Just pretend it's an audition, just go in.'

She sashayed in.

But then she was very single minded, always. It was an all-girls school, I used to call them 'hot house flowers.' They'd all been handpicked at four, and it wasn't whether they'd been primed to write their name or read word cards that some of the demented parents had held up from the moment they could hold up their heads.

No, it was 'potential' and Georgia passed with flying colours. My mother was so excited I'd finally had a girl, she had offered to pay the fees.

Seems although she didn't like me, she loved Georgia.

In fact on arriving at the hospital to see the new offspring, the first thing out of her mouth to me was, 'At least you've done something right for a change.'

Was that praise? Who knew?

Because I'd been told 'No' often in my childhood, I was determined not to repeat this. Problem was, I was so busy being 'not my mother' that maybe I swung too far the other way. So I was good cop, my ex was the strict Victorian father.

But Georgia was pretty steely of her own volition.

People have often told me, what wonderful kids I have. But I don't take a bow, they are their own people, I merely gave them food and shelter, and sometimes a little guidance, when they would listen!

Aged eight, I gave Georgia a birthday cake to take to school to share with her classmates. It was a Friday in June for Miss Gemini!

When I got home, the cake, a little battered but otherwise untouched, was on the table. I was puzzled and perturbed.

'Why is the cake here?'

'The teacher said there wasn't any time to cut it.'

'She said WHAT?'

I wrestled what had happened out of Georgia, who was quite truculent.

Seems she had asked to cut it, and the teacher told her yes, later. Then the other girls began to ask, teacher again said they would cut it later as there was no time.

Finally, the teacher told her 'Bring it back on Monday, we will try and cut it then.'

I was outraged, and sad for Georgia.

I was concerned.

'Are you alright? Are you upset? Everything will be alright. Don't cry.'

'Cry, I didn't cry.'

'OK.'

'I wasn't going to let them see me cry.'

Oh you're so tough, and continue to be so.

Dear darling, Georgia!

Having a daughter was wonderful, having kids was wonderful … and hard work. But a daughter, everybody buys you pink, it was pink on down. My mother approved, mind you she didn't always approve.

Two kids, even though I had the 'matching set' one of each as I liked to call it, didn't feel quite enough. Seems the third one was determined to be there.

I got pregnant with Jacob unintentionally. I was still breastfeeding as Georgia was nine months old, and I thought that protected me. In this case I was wrong.

We had to make some phone calls to give out the great news.

My mother was in Spain on vacation with her best friend. She was not happy, told me off, shouted, told me I was irresponsible. She was away one more week, so we had a little more peace before her return.

David called our great friend and mentor Lewie in San Francisco.

'Lewie, I think I put my foot in it, Elizabeth's pregnant!'

'David, darling, I don't think it was your foot.'

I had found it hard to get pregnant the first time. Then I did a health thing, hair analysis, vitamins and minerals, to clean out the toxins you understand. I was low in zinc, low in calcium, high in some toxins. We both got tested, David was sure I was the problem. Many people have great difficulties getting pregnant. He liked to 'blame'. My mother was anxious for more grandchildren, although

I'm sure she wondered what sort of mother I would make. After three months of my new regime I got pregnant with Georgia.

In those days you didn't ask the sex, and they didn't tell you, it was a surprise! Apparently, a sign the vitamin regime had worked was you produced 'pretty' children.

Georgia wasn't just pretty, she was gorgeous, and strong minded, and artistic, and graceful and smart. I won't belittle myself entirely, but a few things I wasn't.

I wasn't that great at giving birth either. Georgia's birth was the easiest, but then she's a girl, girls are better at most things. Except me, I wasn't much good at anything, according to my mother.

I've got a new favourite programme on TV, about a medium giving readings, and I often wondered what sort of messages my mother would send me from the spirit world, given that most messages are miss you, love you, forgive you and sorry I'm not there. Yes I can wonder. Of course I'm sad she died, sad for many things.

I think when I cried at the news it was shock. Because, however educated you are, however smart, you somehow expect your parents to be around forever. Well I certainly did with my mother even though I had often absented myself from the proceedings.

She said things like 'Over my dead body would I want you to look after me.' After all she had Annie, Annie had been in the family 20 years, started off as a nanny to Philip's kids, then looked after my mother for 10 years.

Sometimes I wanted to say something about how she was looked after, offer help and suggestions don't you know. They were never well received, Annie and I would argue. One particular day we were shouting about something, yes Annie was a good pupil, she had quickly learned the 'Green' way of communicating. We were shouting and furious and I called Tina, in a fit of rage.

'You have to be nice to Annie, what would we do without her?'

How demeaning, seems the maid was more important than me. But then in my life so far, it seems everyone is more important than me. I have a friend who says I did well to survive! Everything was a great fight, the fight for what? The fight was for love, for recognition, for understanding, for acknowledgement, for having a voice and just being me.

Somehow, I never gave up. I have a sticker on my fridge and it says: 'Never, Never, Never give up' attributed to Winston Churchill, and believe me he must have had many times when he wanted to give up.

So I soldier on, after all what doesn't kill you makes you stronger!

I used to think I would just write a book called 'The Sayings of Alma Green' and there were some pretty good ones. But then I also know that your parents shape you and form you, and I heard her mother was a tyrant, tough, passed on down through the female line. Uncle Harold told me she was the odd one out, the boys liked her apparently, but odd one out.

In her 90s she still had a friend from school, Ann. Ann was delightful. On moving day to North London, that bastion of Jewishness, we were sent to Ann's house nearby for the day. I will never forget, we ate jelly in the bath. I was eight, Philip was five, but jelly in the bath! We'd never done that before, nor since I guess.

Was life about to change, get sweeter?

But the problem with 'No' was I didn't use it too much.

After all, I wanted to be liked, and loved and feel up close to someone. All that sex, and not much love.

Reminds me of my coming of age trip to New York. As a treat, finally after miserable times at school and college and in my marriage, it was time to look after me, and find out I could be alone.

It was intoxicating.

I'm in Macy's trying on shoes, and the grey pair of Calvin Klein's are divine. I could still wear 4" heels in those days. I look at others, but this is the pair I want and suddenly it's a familiar feeling. I know I've had this feeling before: shoes are like men, you know straight away.

This trip is a birthday treat, so a July trip for a brave Cancerian, a kind of Israel tour after GCSE's, a belated 21st birthday present. People said I was brave, or were they saying 'crazy' when I wasn't listening! But I'd done some homework, I had a list of restaurants where single women could sit alone at the bar, and eat alone uninterrupted at a table for one. Funny thing was, I didn't, not any night!

I chose the caring sharing Tribeca Grand downtown. They offered flowers, fruit and a goldfish for the room, in case I was lonely. I chose to sleep alone, yes me, the eternally lonely woman. No kids, no dogs, no cooking, no driving and definitely no goldfish.

What am I doing here in New York? I pretended culture and shopping had called me here, but of course men and dating. It was at the time I was writing my Jewish Chronicle column.

So here we are, Elizabeth and the City.

I had, before leaving London, put myself on Jdate as if I was a native New Yorker. I received emails saying 'have I got a match for you' with a never-ending supply of single New Yorkers, many of whom looked quite tasty.

The men listed themselves as adventurous and ready for love, but most of them weren't even up to answering an email!

Except for Scott. He came by the first night and accompanied me and jet lag to dinner in this exciting city. But he was unhappy as he told me at length, and the sight of me did not lift his spirits although I looked pretty good. As we walked back from the restaurant I had to take my high heels off in Canal Street. No, it wasn't the Calvins, just tired feet. He was despairing and after delivering me back to my hotel, managed to walk away, not run. Then he did run, such first night jitters, we were never in contact again.

Next day I became a tourist, explored the city, the shops and the skyscrapers in the sunshine. Night two at Bread, a lovely restaurant next to the hotel I drank watermelon mojitos and met Brad. A glass, just one glass, made the already glossy city positively sparkle and Brad wasn't exactly a stranger. I'd seen him in the hotel reception with his American chiseled chin telling the concierge he had a problem.

Armed with watermelon courage as I sat myself down beside him, I asked him

'What was the problem?'

'Dinner alone.'

'Is that it?' I'm shocked. 'You mind dining alone?'

'I do.'

Hmm I thought that was only a girl problem. Upper hand here? I'm reveling in dining alone and he's upset. OK, I'm here to look after you and he was happy to talk, people in New York like talking, a city after my own heart. They talk and don't pounce like they do in London. We had a great dinner and he walked me the two minutes back to the hotel.

Saturday I met an Israeli man, he really liked to talk, mostly about himself. This trip, was this going to be MY nearly silent trip? He waxed lyrical about his ideal woman, no-one here was shy, nor delicate, was this the city for me?

He outlined all the qualities he was looking for, I am sure I fitted most of them but he didn't notice as I sat in the sun looking delicious. Lucky escape?

I had one old friend in the city, Jim. We'd met on a Landmark course five years earlier and he took me back to the same restaurant on West Broadway we'd dined in five years earlier. How romantic. We laughed, and hugged, and reminisced and then I went home alone. No-one was waiting up for me, to tell me off, or berate me about anything. Just me and a lovely soft bed, all mine!

Next night I discovered a restaurant called Odeon further downtown, which became a firm favourite when I started living here. This trip was a kind of checking out the city, as well as the men. This night I am sitting at the bar, I get more daring the longer I am here. I met George from Uruguay. We talked and drank with a fervor that our lives might depend on and he walked me home. They are gentlemen here and he promised me a future dinner.

Only problem, I'm still waiting.

New York is so carefree, it fitted my mood. It wasn't even about flirting, chatting was good. I made girlfriends, took the subway to Brooklyn for lunch, waved to the Green Lady as I rode the Staten Island Ferry and glanced back fondly at Manhattan through the waves – beautiful even without the Twin Towers gracing the skyline. No wonder my ancestors, some of them, had got off the boat here. Why not you grandpa?

After three days, my youngest Jacob texted me with questions, couldn't shed my mum role quite that easily.

'Sorry, what's the time difference? Is it hot? Did you leave money to buy food? I ordered books off Amazon with your card, is that ok?'

Ha, can manage without me, but not my card. Cupboard love?

I bought him a lilac shirt and confidently texted to ask: 'You do like lilac don't you?'

'What's lilac?' he asked.

Is there no hope for men?

At least there's hope for New York. In fact, the love affair I had was with New York – the men didn't come close.

When I left the hotel the cute doorman left a red rose on my bag. It must be love.

This laid the groundwork for my next adventure, which was closer than I knew.

The Jewish Chronicle ran a version of this entitled 'Not much sex, too much city.'

But now I live here I can redress the balance.

DOCTORS AND REALITY TV

CHAPTER 26

After leaving India, life felt unsettled. Living at Dr. Sharma's the homeopathic doctor, made me feel I belonged somewhere, because I felt like a changeling most of the time. I didn't seem to belong anywhere, either I had been born into the wrong family or they'd come and taken me out of my 'real' mother's crib and put me into a strange crib.

I kept on, every day, looking in all the wrong places, like a hamster on a wheel, round and round in the same loop expecting the outcome to be different. Love was damn devious, difficult to find, and I had pretty much no idea how it looked or felt, or tasted or how it manifested itself.

I had had the same experience after my father died. He was the one on my side, when he wasn't laid out in an armchair dribbling cough sweets or suffering from a migraine.

The day after the funeral I went tearfully into the dining room, I don't remember how my mother seemed to be feeling, I was too consumed with upset and confusion.

'What are we going to do now?' I blurted out.

'Just imagine he's gone out and he's not coming back.'

Sort of like gone shopping I thought.

I hadn't been allowed to go to the burial grounds so I had no kind of closure. For the next 17 years I looked for him everywhere; on buses, at the shops, round corners. He really had 'gone shopping.' Intellectually I knew I wouldn't find him, didn't stop me feverishly looking.

Until, one day I was in Texas visiting an old British boyfriend. Texas hadn't changed him much and we were at odds, until luckily I made friends with new people, jumped ship and stayed with them. One afternoon a thunderbolt landed. Don't know if it was the strange surroundings, the unfamiliar people, but I realised my father was dead, and I was never going to see him again. The enormity of it hit me and I started to cry, there were so many tears to shed. Bless my new friends, they were there, letting me cry and not interfering with the process.

After several hours, I rubbed my red swollen eyes, grimaced slightly, stood up and stretched. It was over as surprisingly as it had begun. My father was dead, and I missed him. I cried for not knowing him well enough, I cried that he'd been ill mostly, for his pill taking, for his short life. I cried for many things that day in Dallas.

But then one night while I was living at Dr. Sharma's house on Seymour Place I decided to take a stand, a stand for a better future for myself. Adrian Love, DJ on Capital Radio, had invited me a few times to go and listen to his show. This time I was going to go to meet Anna Raeburn, agony aunt extraordinaire and the Capital Doctor, and listen to them give advice on air to people's problems. Then I would talk to Colin, the Capital doctor and get him to listen to my problems.

I couldn't approach him inside the studio, so I kissed Adrian goodbye, shook hands with the others and ostensibly left. In truth I was waiting on the windy blustery corner of Euston Road to waylay the Doctor and ask him for help.

He was heading for nearby Euston train station, I didn't have much time to make my pitch.

'My dear, come with me to the train station, we can grab a cup of tea and talk there, out of the wind.'

I had nothing else better to do, so I followed him along the road.

'What's wrong?'

We talked for a few minutes and he seemed friendly and warm. He was friendly and warm because his proposal had nothing to do with talking me through a few problems. His solution was to come to Sharma's house before next week's broadcast and … fuck my problems away.

Boy, I had not seen this one coming.

He was a plump, friendly English doctor, British to the core. When he wasn't sorting out people's problems in a big Northampton hospital he was playing soldiers in the Territorial Army, and believe me he was pretty good at 'standing to attention.'

Funny, this was the solution I'd always sought before, now, offered on a plate took the mystery and intrigue away. Was it that I liked to be the chief protagonist and seductress? It seemed a pretty good idea with limits and boundaries, nothing to hope and wish for or be wistful about.

I'm in London, he's in Northampton, married, working, comes to London most weeks on a Wednesday. I could be the fill-in between tea and broadcasting. Best offer I'd had lately. I took it.

I'm not a person who likes rules. In fact my only rule in life is, there are no rules. Ask my family if I've ever followed the rules, they will tell you 'No', pretty much not! So the Doctor and I had a steamy time together while my life was unraveling around me.

Meanwhile, my brother was about to meet the woman who would become his wife and produce his two beautiful children, Georgia and Jacob's sometime playmates.

I had beaten him to it, I had started on children already, and all of us now took part in the ultimate anti-rules show.

Filming the reality TV show 'Trust Me I'm a Teenager' was like having a party for two weeks. Three teenagers scrutinised us, put up with our behavior, and then dived in and changed it.

My husband hated the filming, so he said, as he sat each night drinking with the crew when the filming was finished. I'm not a drinker, something he was always pointing out to me petulantly, finally the red wine flowed as he sat with his new buddies. No, I was not a drinker. Aged 18, I'd been a barmaid, drunk my ten vodka and orange juices a night, then walked home alone, down Fitzjohn's

Avenue from Hampstead, floating and fearless.

Now the drinking began at home.

But I got the mornings. The crew would arrive at 6am to film us getting up, getting three kids ready for school. One morning they gave Simon a megaphone, which he enjoyed too much as he screamed into Jacob's top bunk.

'Wake up, wake up, time to get up!' Good coming from the guy who was terrible at getting up, seems he was better at getting other people up.

It didn't go down well and the morning I made scrambled eggs for everyone, crew included, prompted a huge jealous tantrum from David, which was all caught on camera, with a beautiful shot of the cat Patchy looking on in bemusement.

A star was born. Or was it just me? I loved the attention, and my favourite spot was the Camcorder situated in the small front living room, my purple room. There is a fabulous shot of me trying to work the controls on it, to complain about my day, except it's already working and there's a shot of me peering into the camera perplexed and pissed off.

So Channel 4 came to dinner, to interview us and vet us. They loved us, what's not to love? Big family, chaotic household, yes I did try tidying up a little, but the three cats, the three kids, an au pair and David made a mess. David, Mr perfect Virgo, I am sure would not agree with me. Seems I'm the messy one. After dinner, they left a questionnaire for me to fill in, many questions, taxing my concentration, shot from running this crazy household. One of the questions was 'What do you think of rules?'

As I wrote the answer I immediately thought to myself: I DON'T do rules.

The ONLY rule I have is that there are no rules and the premise of the show is 'Rules.'

The teenagers got to examine the house from top to toe before delivering a heavy critique and telling us how it was going to be, for the next week.

'Why do you need an au pair?' Sammy aged 15, asked 'if you don't work?'

Can't answer.

'How would you describe your relationship with your husband?' she asked.

I lean forward, almost conspiratorially: 'Do you know what the word 'volatile' means?'

Anyway, the au pair got the week off and I get a job in the local café serving food, and I guess the house cleaned itself.

Amazingly, some of the rules stuck. Bedtimes were abolished, forever. I had to do more cleaning and a good time was had by all. Perhaps not David!

A few days before transmission, Jonathon the director came round, he was so cute, and I had a huge 'crush' on him. He was sweating.

'I do hope you like what I've done, I'm going to sit down with you and watch it.'

I wasn't too surprised. He had made the programme with love. I shouted a lot and we lived in chaos, it wasn't untidy chaos, it wasn't dirty chaos, just living with kids who I had always hoped and wanted to be self-expressed.

They were. Jonathan portrayed it perfectly.

There was a touching scene where Simon, my wonderful eldest, cooked us a romantic Valentine's dinner. This was lovely because the rest of the time he spent prone on the sofa. After all, being nearly 18 was very tiring, although he did have some health issues to contend with.

Yes, me and rules have had a long contentious stand-off.

I'M COMING TO AMERICA:
CUE NEIL DIAMOND

CHAPTER 27

Three Continents.

This is the perfect weekend to discuss.

As I sit alone in bed.

I've eaten all the bad stuff, food that is, last night. It doesn't taste all that nice. I have a way that usually works. I ask myself: why do you need to eat ice cream and cookies … again? After all, I know how they taste, don't need to keep doing it.

But last night I did.

Moving to New York was wanted and needed and brave. So people tell me, for once I was just determined, in spite of the US government seemingly not wanting immigrants.

I've always been good at going where I'm not wanted. This is a perfect example. After long visa proceedings, you pay expensive lawyer's fees, a fee to the US government and then finally at the end you are summoned to the US Embassy in London, in Grosvenor Square.

You have to leave your mobile phone and keys behind. The nearby chemist shop is making a fortune storing them for all the visa applicants.

We lined up in the street, thank God it wasn't raining. Every nationality, gender, size, age; eat your heart out Donald Trump. The person next to me had won a green card in the Lottery, Chinese in origin, she had come to firm up her paperwork.

There was much to attend to. Your passport had to have at least six months on it. Mine was nearly expiring when I started the process, so I got a new one. Then they wanted to know why I had a new passport!

We sat inside a huge hall, probably 300 people, holding tickets. All around were machines hanging from the ceiling showing numbers. You had to concentrate to see which number applied to the queue you were in. I was called to the first window quite promptly and handed over some papers.

Then I sat down again for another hour or so. Someone told me Superman, Henry Cavill, had been there the day before, just sitting with the people in the hall. That may have made it a little more exciting.

The last window asked for money, they were curt and abrupt and asked questions.

'Why do you want to live in New York?'

'Because I love it there.'

Don't mention love or romance, US customs are not on the side of romance.

'You like animals, I see you have a dog, what will happen to him?'

'He will be looked after.'

I don't feel welcome yet, but I keep smiling.

Other questions follow, all gruff. Finally,

'OK, here are your papers. Thank you very much.'

I want to whoop, but I maintain strict dignity and march outside 'til I can celebrate. Something I wanted came true.

This was the easy bit, like giving birth. Having the baby, easy, bringing it up never-ending.

I had been travelling in and out of New York for a few years, usually through Newark airport until someone told me they were more pleasant at JFK. Well damn they couldn't have been much nastier.

Then came the special revelatory moment, with my newly appointed passport, with its newly appointed visa, ink barely dry, I was ushered through as a trusted business person.

'Right hand.'

'OK left hand.'

'Look into the camera.'

I'm holding my breath, trying to concentrate, even though it's the middle of the night where I have come from. Here in New York, finally at JFK, it's early evening.

I made it. I'm in.

Now the hard part begins, I have to make a life, feel like I belong. Yes, now there's only me to look after in my small one-bedroom apartment. I've left behind a four bedroom house in London, with my car on the drive. In Manhattan, it would be easy to drive. The streets run in straight lines. Not like where I've come from in Hampstead, North London, with its winding roads and hidden street signs where, of course, we drive on the other side of the road.

I'm not familiar with the New York streets, nor the subway. The buses in New York, and the subways are a puzzle. Some have no maps, some change lines. It's Saturday afternoon and I'm taking the C train, I swipe my unlimited ticket and go down to the platform. Yes, I'm going in the right direction, uptown, but when the train arrives … it's an 'F' train. I strain to hear the train announcer, who says 'This is an F train, going on the C line to 59th where it will then go express.'

Express to where? Yes I've jumped on regular trains that then speed through 6 stops and deposit me 3 stops out of my way. Tourists don't be of faint heart, we've all been downtown to Brooklyn, even over the bridge when we're trying to go the other way. Of course it's a breathtaking view going over the bridge, but only takes your breath away when you realise there isn't a river crossing between you and home. So I concentrated on the subways. Didn't use buses for two years, and the East side, forget it, took me even longer.

Small children, that's what you needed on a Saturday. We joined the rice cake brigade, up in Highgate, North London. I remember taking the children to see their first puppet show there, they also had live performances, with actors. I was ready to leave the housework behind, jump in the car and go to the shows, week after week at Lauderdale House. With my bag of rice cakes! Afterwards, we could run in the park, down to the pond, see the ducks. It was a grand sweeping park. We were on the hill but the lawns swept down, down to the ponds, then home for lunch.

I had a sticker on my fridge in East Finchley, it was a joke.....of course? Or was it?

'WHEN I MARRIED MR. RIGHT

I DIDN'T KNOW

HIS MIDDLE NAME WAS ALWAYS.'

Haha, I married Mr. Virgo and to drag him away from his routine, leave something unwiped to go out was not looked upon well, causing upset, in fact, screaming usually resulted. All the more reason to rebel, I liked to rebel.

I was in control when they were small. Soon they were all taller than me and could answer me back. Simon liked sleeping on the couch, Georgia painted pictures, then painted herself.

Jacob was under Simon's control. So he heard the filthy jokes, the swear words, and Jacob listened well. The year Jacob was eight he did 10 commercials. He earned so much money that he had to pay income tax that year.

The Evening Standard newspaper came to Hereward House, his private somewhat prissy prep school, to take his picture and do a full-page spread. Leone Sampson, the headmistress, didn't seem to mind, her prior career was actress. She understood being in the public eye, so we didn't have to be too posh and shun the limelight.

They stood him up against a stack of Encyclopedia Britannica volumes, and wrote about him in the paper. He was grinning and cheeky. He wore his school uniform grey V-neck sweater with navy school stripe on the neck, grey flannels and navy striped tie. It was a boys' prep school, expensive and privileged, hopefully a stepping stone to a good job and good standing in the world. Only boys attended, it was cosy and comforting. The parents had to take it in turn to help the little boys out of their cars in the morning because in suburban Swiss Cottage there was usually nowhere to park. It was hard for some of the mums to part with their beloveds and hand them over to another mum, occasionally dads and always a prefect.

I remember one morning doing duty with Joe, brother of one of Georgia's best friends. We ushered in a small boy and Joe leaned down oh so solicitously and asked, 'Are you OK?'

The small boy looked up sweetly and trustingly, 'Hello Joe, I'm fine.'

The five-year-old and the 10-year-old were so kind to each other. It was a wonderful way to start the day, for me anyway. No division, no rank, just care and concern. It was a very nurturing place and did my boys well.

Mothering was the thing I did best, and consumed my life. School runs and driving dominated, washing clothes, cooking meals, I was a stay-at-home mum. If I'd had a wonderful career I'd left, I would have continued it, but I didn't. I stayed home and helped with homework, and tried to make moments special. So we went to auditions, the boys tap danced and did karate. They all did painting classes, acting classes, the North London mania to fill up every night after school.

Every week my mother said, 'Boys don't dance, why are they doing dancing?'

Lucky it wasn't ballet I guess, and then we started going on holiday. We went camping in France, with French Country Camping, and met Phil and Hazel, an older couple who were our couriers.

We stayed in a tent, a big already erected tent with three 'rooms' at the back, with beds and a rail to hang clothes on, flaps in front that zipped up. Yes, this was comfortable camping. There was a living space with a table and chairs, we moved them outside the tent immediately upon arrival. So much French fresh air was wonderful. Every morning when we woke up, late, the tent would be full of children crayoning and chatting and hanging out.

Camping was brilliant. The kids could run around by themselves, safely, which they did in a huge posse. We were in Brittany. The weather wasn't wonderful, but the patisserie was.

To take a shower or wash up, you had to walk to the shower block. It was fun, an adventure. We were so excited we kept recommending camping to anyone who would listen, but people were squeamish.

'No shower? No running water? Are you crazy?'

No, we had great conversations at the shower block, made new friends, seemed to be the heart of the camp site! Plans were made there for the following day, outings arranged, confidences exchanged, in many languages!

Meanwhile, friends and family went camping and rented trailers with running water, oh so hot in the heat of France.

Simon taught Jacob a joke to tell at auditions.

'So Jacob you ask them … what's the difference between a hedgehog and a BMW? Hedgehogs have pricks on the outside …

Usually, he didn't have to complete it, people loved it and laughed. It sounded so cute coming out of the mouth of an eight year old, so all the hard-bitten executives thought.

Then Simon coached him a bit more.

'Make sure you ask whoever you're talking to … what car do you drive? If they say BMW, you tell the joke and make it about Mercedes.'

It obviously worked, he got lots of work, and plenty of money. Georgia and Jacob had investments by the time they were 12.

So I hold Saturdays and Sundays as precious, family time. Yes, soon they got older and weren't interested, but I had them for a precious moment.

Here in New York City I can go a whole day without speaking to anyone. Sometimes I yearn for just a 'good morning'. I can see the sun from my windows, and the spires of the cathedral. Yes, I'm lucky I have trees and spires outside my window, I'm in the grounds of St. John the Divine, one of the largest Anglican cathedrals in the world, I could be in the Oxfordshire countryside.

When I first got here, Hugh was one of my only friends, and bonus, he had a family which was familiar and comforting for me. I hung out with his kids, while he went to Long Island to see his girlfriend Annie, I looked after Bobby the youngest, fed him, bought food and cleaned. I even slept in Hugh's bed when he wasn't there, to be close to him. God, I was so deluded.

When he took everyone to Coney Island, he brushed me off.

'I'm so sorry, honey, no room in the car, but why don't we talk while I'm driving and you can give me directions.'

I knew it was wrong, and demeaning, but I somehow reasoned the bad feelings away and did it anyway. Anything for a bit of human contact, although it hurt that I wasn't invited or included. Wasn't contact, of any kind, however mean spirited better than no contact? Don't answer!

Later he showed me pictures. He was my Svengali, he had me under his spell. It took a lot to break the spell, and sometimes he was nice. His mixed messages made it confusing.

One Saturday, he invited me to brunch with him and his kids, at a diner on Amsterdam Avenue. We were meeting Jerry and his kids, their oldest girls, both 16 were besties. It was like the mums meeting, only it was the dads. We were already a large noisy group, doing exactly what you did on a Saturday, and, bonus, I'm in New York.

Yes I still pinch myself.

Jerry came into the diner and sat beside me. When he heard my English accent he told me: 'I went to boarding school in England.'

'Really, where did you go?'

'I went to Carmel College in Oxfordshire.'

'REALLY?'

'Yes, why?'

'Because that's where my brother went to school.'

'Who's your brother?'

When I told him we all gasp and start to laugh.

'No, what a small world. He was two years below me at school.'

'Would he know you?'

'Probably not. I remember him. We used to have a card game going on in the cupboard behind the coat room and he was the runner.'

'The runner?'

'Yes.'

'Wow.'

'Now of course I just read about him in the newspaper.'

'Wow.'

I can't think of anything else to say, what a small world. Then we start to talk about why I'm here and I tell him I'm looking for a business to buy in order to come and live in New York.

'You should look on Businessesforsale.com.'

I did, I always tell people that when I tell the story. That's where I found my business, so I bless you and curse you in the same breath, Jerry.

At this time I'm just craving Hugh's attention, not ready to look for my business. But this is useful information. My empty days and nights are focused around Hugh!

I met Hugh on Jdate, after I'm done with him I never go back on Jdate. I'm on a few other dating sites, I tell Hugh, after all no point in waiting for something I can't have, and sometimes am not sure I want.

We're in a cab one night, he's dropping me off on a date, he's going to his therapist. There won't be any difference after the session, I don't know what they do there but nothing changes. I think he tells her his latest theories and then persuades her to accept them. My would-be date calls me up.

'So sorry I'm just going to be a little late.'

Hugh is listening intently, is he jealous? He grabs the phone and starts ranting at the poor guy. Tells him it's not acceptable behaviour, frightens him off and then, pleased with himself, hands the phone back to me.

In a fury I tell him: 'Stop the cab, drop me off, I don't want to be with you one moment longer. Goodbye'

But then of course I relent and a day or so later, I'm waiting and crying by the phone. Until one night I go drinking cocktails with a girlfriend, I'm such a lightweight drinker, two cocktails, somehow for once they light up my reason or is it unreason? I decide it's time, partly fuelled by the fact that I met someone else, equally unsuitable it will transpire, I decide it's time to undo Hugh, dispose of him, say goodbye, give him the heave ho.

I call him when I get home, fuelled by Dutch courage.

His daughter answers the phone and tries to stall me. Sophia doesn't like me. On a trip to the movies I treated her to, she lectured me on how unsuitable I am for her dad!

I insist I have to speak to him, I can hear him in the background grumbling reluctantly.

'Hi, what do you want?'

'Hugh, I don't want to see you any more, I don't want us to be in touch. We're done, this is goodbye.'

Even in my alcohol-fuelled mood, I stop to hear what he has to say. He's spluttering.

'Oh no, I knew this was coming. Ok, are you sure?'

'Yes, goodbye.' I put the phone down.

What a relief. It means a lot more alone time, but the price was too high. Bullying is unacceptable.

I sit and cry on Sundays, angry tears, angry at my exploitation.

It's early days in my New York life, I'm not a business owner yet, I'm just a lonely woman living alone in New York.

Before my divorce I had three children, three cats, two dogs, an au pair and a husband, and a partridge in a pear tree by the sound of it. Now it's just me, and long distance kids. It's my time.

GIVING BIRTH, OUCH!

CHAPTER 28

Pregnancy. My forte.

My strength. I was still seeing Dr. Sharma when I got pregnant with Simon. I was careful and eating clean. I weighed less after his birth than my starting weight. YESSS!

I was the designated pregnant driver as I wasn't drinking. I painted the bedroom ceiling on a ladder, eight months pregnant and counting. I was wonderful, until the birth.

My ex was scared, I'm telling you he was scared. At the birth, he stood by my head, he was not brave. He would pass out at the dentist, so he told me, because in all the time I'd known him he'd never been once to the dentist.

His mother never took him either, judging by the state of his teeth. He had rabbit front teeth, we had to get them fixed, they were ugly and protruding and made it hard to eat. My dentist filed them down and capped them, and I don't think he fainted once. Sedatives are wonderful.

I'm a little five footer, size four feet, that indicates small hips. I think you need bigger feet to have child bearing hips, and then I tried to deliver this monster.

Simon was 8lbs 11oz. I hadn't seen my feet for the last month or so. He sat on my bladder, so I was uncomfortable and getting a seat on the Tube wasn't always easy. Women offer other women seats, many of the men sat tight. You know who you are! I worked up until three weeks before the birth. I worked for my ex in his office in Soho, my mother came in and did the accounts. We were above the Italian deli, round the corner from the porn shops and peep shows. Madame Jojos was just along the street, the transvestite bar.

One night I saw a bunch of beautiful women walking along the street, bejeweled in splendid frocks, I was too far away to see their Adam's apples bobbing in the moonlight. But I could hear the deep voices, it was a shock.

The labour started well enough, my best friend, Marcia was there, I was afraid, and once the contractions started, we had this joke.

'I've changed my mind, I'm coming back tomorrow.' It was the most inevitable process I'd ever found myself in. I liked to have an out in things, a back door. There was no back door here, I was fully committed if not fully dilated. It went very slowly, I walked and talked and joked for as long as I could. Marcia and I paced the corridors until it was nearly midnight. Things were moving slowly and it was mightily painful, I decided to have an epidural, which had seemed like a good idea, until they put the needle in too far and it turned into a lumbar puncture.

Even with all that medical intervention, I could still feel every contraction, even with my back to the monitor. It was a long, painful night, thank God I knew it would end in a beautiful baby. I didn't even know what I was having, in those days they were reluctant to tell you, in case they got it wrong although in England we didn't sue.

So I laboured along, literally, it seemed never ending.

'I want to push.'

'Push, push,' Marcia and David were a chorus. I was screaming.

'It feels like I want to take a shit.'

'That's great, keep pushing.'

At the last moment, the doctor came in with a huge metal contraption, a Ventouse, to suction the baby out. I screamed, and tore. Marcia told me later the doctor had his foot on the end of the bed, to give him some traction.

'It was bloody. The veins were standing out on the doctor's head. David was nearly fainting.'

Marcia had had a little girl, Sharni, a few months earlier, so she knew what it felt like. Harder than anything you can imagine, more painful and intense than anyone could tell you, and relentless ending, in this urge to push as if you were going to the loo, but I wasn't on the toilet, so inhibiting.

Maybe the stress of being pulled out so aggressively created some stress for him in later life. His head was pointed and out of shape from his ordeal, and his Apgar was one, should be nine or ten, that meant his breathing was barely there, thank God my consciousness was barely there. They whisked him away to the special baby unit and for three days I was on my back, from the lumbar puncture effect, they had inefficiently put the epidural needle in too far.

I breast-fed him, they just brought him and put him on my boob, and then took him away to change his nappy while I could only lay there. I was so sore, my back hurt so badly.

The doctor came round the ward.

'Will my back recover?'

'Should be fine in a few days, I know you're very uncomfortable.'

I can't imagine how he knew, he never gave birth. Doctorspeak no doubt.

Marcia went to see the baby in the special baby unit.

'He's looks so funny, next to all the tiny preemie babies. But his Apgar came up, his breathing is fine.'

My brother came to see me, which was startling. I was in the public ward of the Whittington Hospital, which served a poor area of North London. It was my local hospital and there we were, once I'd had the baby I was put into a ward with at least 20 beds. Opposite me, I remember were the 'frummers' (religious Jews).

They had huge families, I wasn't sure what number baby she was on, but she would close the curtain every night to take off her sheitel (wig) and put on a headscarf. I knew what she was doing, I'm not sure some of the other patients did, probably not the Indian family squatting on the bed next to mine eating their chapattis and Indian vegetables. It was a melting pot in Archway, North London.

My brother doesn't like hospitals, the poverty of the ward wasn't the thing that made him uncomfortable, just the hospital itself. The smell, the rubber floors, this was an old 19th century building, the smells must have been lingering there for a hundred years or more.

He was carrying a wonderful monkey who sat on a child-sized wicker chair with a fan back. Monkey is still in my house now.

After three days I could sit up and go home. Marcia and I now spoke every day, I was determined to breast feed, but this was all new to me. My mother seemed quite excited, and I named him after everyone in best Jewish tradition.

Simon was my late father's name. Andrew was in honour of Annette, Auntie Netty, Ethan in honour of Ephraim my late grandfather, on my mother's side. I had done my homework, and taken this seriously.

Georgia was much different. The labour was painful, but shorter and sweeter, then this little bundle of gorgeousness came out. It was summer, we sat in the garden, she rolled on a rug. She was number two, now I knew what to do, except I had a three year old running around.

But two was manageable, after all, I had two hands. A friend of mine reckoned three kids needed three parents, so at two, theoretically, I should be able to manage.

MORE OF MY BROTHER

CHAPTER 29

Relationships, so hard to get right, yet the thing I most want to get right, so I've never stopped trying.

In one of my dating column pieces I wrote for The Jewish Chronicle, the opening sentence said: 'I was brought up in a cold climate and I don't mean the weather.'

My editor wanted to know more.

I replied, 'I think that says everything you need to know, after all, less is more.'

My marriage didn't produce the result I wanted either.

I'm sitting here watching the adverts on TV, watching these perfect households they create for 30 seconds on TV. I'm wondering, what it would be like to wake up every morning contented, free, self-expressed and loved. Yes, I want the white picket fence, now I'm nearly American, I want the American dream.

Seems I never want to give up searching, I've learned a lot along the way.

Everything that happened, did it really happen that way? Now I've put my spin on it, added my grown up feelings, pretended I knew my mother and father's feelings, yes I remembered to add my father, that mystery absent figure.

All that food I refused when I was three. Was I making an early protest? Did I know my all-important, all-consuming brother was on the way? Of course not, I didn't know anything.

Sometimes I say to Rita, my friend and mentor, listener and inspiration: 'I just want to be normal, ordinary. Why can't I have a close family? I wanted a loving mother and father, that ship has sailed. Now I just want my brother and sister-in-law, nieces, nephews and a great nephew, but it seems I don't have that either. Why me? Why not?'

All those unanswerable questions!

My friends ask me why my brother doesn't want me around, doesn't want to talk to me, have me in his life.

'What happened? What did you do?' Seems I'm the one in the wrong, of course.

I've racked my brains. Did something happen? Did I say something terrible? He always shouts at me, he's curt and abrupt, if I question it, I'm told 'He's like that with everyone.'

'I'm not everyone.'

He answers the phone 'Hello. Yes, what do you want? No ... OK, goodbye.'

I know he called my mother every morning, this is how the conversation went:

'Hello ma, are you alright?'

'Yes.'

'Is there anything you need?'

'No, nothing.'

'Alright, goodbye.'

Later in life, I told her when he asked if there's anything she needs, to say 'Yes, I need you to come and see me.'

She didn't. Funny family, asking was not OK.

Is he hurting? If he is, I can't go help him, talk about it with him. It's enough to be with my own hurt. Philip was sent away to boarding school aged eight. Did he make that mean he wasn't wanted? Was he lonely? Did it cause an irreparable rift between him and the rest of the family? I found out many years later, they were going to send me to boarding school too. So my mother could be a businesswoman, her calling in life. But they didn't send me. I was at home with the nanny, the nanny who shouted! But he was revered, the centre of her life, Jewish son in a Jewish family, the successful son. Oy vay!

You only had to go to the 'Philip Green shrine' in my mother's flat to experience that. She lived in a high ceilinged mansion flat in Maida Vale, with long corridors. The walls were lined with newspaper cuttings of him, pictures too. On the rare occasions he visited her, Annie told me he used to like reading all the newspaper cuttings. Then he would look around. My mother was a collector, and I don't mean of anything precious.

Her favourite outing was to go up the main road to Church Street market. All the traders knew her, the chemist was her friend, I guess spending what she did at his shop, she deserved to be his friend. I met him at her birthday dinner one year.

He was Indian, I've always said Jews and Indians are so similar, he obviously thought so too. He told me how much she reminded him of his mother. Jewish mothers, Indian mothers, mothers, all in the same mould, loved and revered their successful sons. He was a pharmacist who owned a chain of chemists' shops, not as many shops as my brother's retail empire.

She had a mantelpiece full of tiny clocks.

She had a special set of shelves full of tiny teapots, in many different shapes, with the names on. One says 'Green & Co'. Another one is shaped like a double decker red bus.

There are tiny shoes on a separate set of shelves.

Then there are the dolls. The beautiful hand-knitted ones, she hand knitted herself, the plastic ones, every kind. She had even taken back the doll collection of my childhood, dolls in costumes from different countries. They took over every surface, the chairs, the armchairs. There was just the sofa left to sit on, and a huge stuffed tiger sat on the back of it, his paws hanging on your head as you sat.

Philip bought a small department store chain called BHS, my mother loved to visit the Oxford Circus store, the premier location, at least two or three times a week. She sat in the café and 'held court,' several of the employees would meet and greet and attend to her. Even they called her 'Gran.' At home, Annie answered the phone, 'Hello, Granny Green's residence.' Friends came to visit her at the store, even I went there, we drank tea and ate cake. She was their biggest customer. Annie came a close second. The Christmas shop at BHS was the biggest temptation of the year. All those quirky toys, and sweets, and smellies, that you never found any other time.

Sometimes, Philip would be there, and he'd come by and say hello. Those were special days for her.

They had Christmas candles, cards, cosmetics and most of all, cuddly toys in all sizes. That's where the tiger came from.

Her flat had a lot of clutter, organised clutter.

One rare day he visited her at her flat and said to Annie in wonder and bemusement: 'Where does all this crap come from Annie darling?'

'From your store Sir,' Annie said without missing a beat.

Annie called everyone Sir and Madam, it wasn't really connected to his title.

He laughed.

One time, Annie left her in bed and ran out of the flat to go to the nearby shop.

'Gran, stay in bed don't get up, I will be back in a few minutes.'

Even Annie called her Gran, I think it was her leading role, the role she played most proudly.

Anyway, not being a person who liked to be told what to do, she got herself out of bed to get the newspaper from the kitchen. The kitchen door was a swing door and she didn't have enough strength to hold it, needless to say it swung on to her head and blood started gushing.

Annie came back and there she was, gashed and bleeding lying on the floor. Annie was panicked, she had deserted her post. I wasn't going to tell anyone she went out, but I wasn't there of course, otherwise this drama would never have arisen.

Philip was summoned and he met her and Annie at the nearby hospital, St. Mary's at Praed Street in Paddington. The head injury was almost forgotten in the excitement of seeing her son because, although they spoke every day, they didn't meet so often.

It almost made the crack on the head OK, well, almost. He told her off and the hospital patched her up and sent her home. It was late into the night.

Next day at lunchtime, Tina called to say she'd had an accident.

'Oh my God what happened?' I was a little concerned.

'She's all right, she's resting, this happened last night.'

'Last night! But it's lunchtime. Why didn't anyone tell me?'

'We didn't want to worry you. She said not to worry you.'

Oh so it was a collusion to leave me out, this was not new, and never got old. I was often left out of the equation. Did I cause it? Was I to blame? Always felt like it!

The kids used to do auditions for photo shoots and commercials. Jacob did a West End play 'Waiting for Godot' when he was eight, he had a big year that year. Georgia had done a BBC TV kids series, when she was eight. I would have to grab them from school and run to town. We got to know the photographers, and agents often in hidden away parts of the West End. It's a jumble of streets, hard to find these places sometimes.

One particular day I parked the car in the Green's drive in St. John's Wood to take the bus into town. It was easier than finding a meter, it was in the days before you could feed the meter from your mobile phone. Besides, I had to be prepared, there was a lot to think about. They were tired, I had to make sure I had snacks with me, and they looked their best. Georgia decided early on about the audition process.

One time after an audition she said to me: 'If they don't pick me it doesn't mean they don't like me, it just means they probably wanted someone with red hair.'

Oh Georgia, teach me to have such wisdom and grace, and not take things personally, that thing I've done my whole life.

When someone tells you something, something critical, something derogatory, not nice, it says more about them than you … it's got nothing to do with you. It's about them, a lesson my daughter realised aged eight.

So we popped into the Green's house on Avenue Road, just to say hi and let them know we were parked outside on their driveway. On this particular early evening, just inside the front door were trays and trays and trays of small white flowering plants.

'What are the flowers for?' I asked Chloe, my small niece.

'They're for the wedding.'

I didn't ask any more questions, we were late and even I realised that if I didn't already know about it, then probably I shouldn't ask.

But I did ask a few days later. I asked my mother.

'It's Philip and Tina's wedding. They are having their marriage blessed by a rabbi in the house.'

'So what are all the flowers for?'

'They are for the chuppah. Tina found a document that shows her grandmother was Jewish, so now the rabbi is going to bless them.'

'So why aren't I invited?' No point in beating about the bush.

'It's only very small. Only me and all her kids are going to be there, only family.'

WHAT? Aren't I family, I'm thinking.

'I'm family, but I'm not invited?'

'You'll have to ask Philip and Tina, it's out of my hands.'

'But I'm your daughter, didn't you ask them why I wasn't invited?'

'Not to do with me. You ask.'

She knew the answer, it was obvious.

So a few days later, I phoned Tina and asked.

'Philip is embarrassed if there are a lot of people, so he's keeping it down to a bare minimum.'

HA! Believe that, you'll believe anything.

In those days, I must have been thick-skinned, can't believe that, am I stupid or a glutton for punishment? Take your pick.

A few days later, I'm walking the dogs down Summerlee Avenue to reach Cherry Tree Woods, and I decide this is a good moment to phone Philip, because really, ironically, there is never a good moment to phone Philip. I ask, ridiculously, why I'm not invited.

He retorts: 'Because I don't want you there. You're not invited, you're a pest, you talk too much. So you won't be there.'

It was like somehow I needed to hear it, to really hear it. THE TRUTH. In case I wasn't sure, didn't know it. He didn't want me around.

I asked them, any one of the three, my mother, my brother and my sister-in-law, persistently for three weeks if I could be at the wedding.

I didn't go.

My mother was so annoyed I kept asking, she decided not to speak to me for the next three weeks.

So the wedding blessing came … and went, and then it was Philip's birthday and we were invited.

A kind gesture? No, probably just to keep the peace? There wasn't any peace. Actually, I think my mother asked him to invite us, a sop, and we had to go. I'd made such a fuss about the wedding that now I was invited I had no choice. I had to go. David was annoyed with me as well, for making such a fuss about everything. But he insisted we go to the birthday party.

I took a deep breath and we went. They had a transvestite magician. He/she was called 'Fay Presto,' funny hey?

As we were taking some food and mingling, uncomfortably, feeling like the poor relations, Chloe said to Georgia: 'My dad pays for you, you know.'

FOOD – THE ENEMY

CHAPTER 30

I found something out this weekend. Me, the lonely one.

Actually, I'm never alone. I'm always with food. Food is like alcohol for me, like drugs, I have an addictive personality. I'm an all-or-nothing girl. I can go out of control at the drop of a hat.

And I've dropped a few hats.

Food is like a wayward lover, a romance gone bad.

I went to a Buddhist 'mindfulness day' where mindful eating worked, for those precious moments it worked. Take a forkful, put it in your mouth, put the fork down. Chew, chew many, many times. Think about where the food came from, who grew it, chew some more. Only then pick up the fork, fill it again, chew some more, repeat, repeat.

In silence!

Well the silence is easy, specially in the evenings when I'm home alone. This is my beautiful American existence and, boy, it can be lonely.

I've started walking, exercise walking. It gives you room to eat.

I'm a binger. In London, Marks and Spencer is the big temptation. Don't you know how it goes? I have my favourite chocolate, favourite cakes, biscuits and sweets. Here, in New York it's pumpernickel bagels, Magnolia Bakery's Banana Cream Pudding and vanilla cupcakes with pink or blue icing. Favourite ice cream shop Amorino, favourite flavour, amarena, with black cherries on the top! Wholefood favourites are Jarlsberg cheese, theirs is so creamy and the pay-by-the-pound cookie bar – can't walk past it!

I like buying food, don't always eat it. Same with books, I choose the best covers, don't always read them all the way through.

Crazy habits.

Not a huge eater, so I tell myself. Eyes bigger than my stomach, my mother delivered this mantra to me as a child.

I always had a dance with food, now I own a restaurant, and how poetic to buy a restaurant that serves meat. Sometimes, I would confide in people: 'I don't eat meat and I own a burger bar.'

That always caused merriment.

'You own a burger bar and you don't eat meat?'

'I don't eat meat. Don't like it.'

But I tasted the burgers, three bites in three years. After all, wasn't this a funny idea to serve meat with bread, washed down with Coca Cola, all my principles around food going out of the window in one go.

Then I developed a serious habit. I binged and purged. I have no idea how it started and I'm not very good at it and not very regular at it either thank God! Sometimes, it's once a year, sometimes once a week. Self-acceptance is very hard.

Now I just binge on sugar, and let it lay on my hips, uncharted. Last time I flew in from London with chocolate bars for gifts I ate them all, in the middle of the night I landed. Jet-lagged and couldn't sleep!

Before leaving Manhattan for London I'd done a juice fast, nothing but homemade juices for two weeks. I hardly cheated, no honestly, after all who am I cheating? Myself? The juice man wrote a cookbook, easy enough even for me, so next I cooked and got healthy and felt good.

I've done so many diets. When I was 18, my diet-obsessed mother sent me to Tyringham Hall. It looked like a Fellini movie set. It was a gracious manor set in huge grounds just outside Newport Pagnell in Buckinghamshire. The people gliding around all day in their dressing gowns made it exotic, a little unexpected in the English countryside. After a few days fasting, no one felt exotic. As we convened in the dining room at every meal to drink a glass of hot water with lemon added, it tasted like the nectar of the gods.

Then we had treatments, had to do something to pass the day. A Scottish douche, jets of alternate hot and cold water being jetted up and down my spine to stimulate the nervous system. I was 18, a little plump, but without realising, nearly perfect in many peoples' eyes, except my mother's. We were massaged, we walked, but the best exercise of all turned out to be sex!

I met Les, middle-aged and away from his wife, and quite sexy. The more I starved, the more we fed each other's appetite and I'm sure it helped me lose weight. Les too!

I lost 10 lbs, thanks for your contribution, Les. I'm sure your wife never knew!

London is my shopping city. I get to go to Topshop, Philip's iconic store, lucky me, yes really, and sometimes I can squeeze into some size 10s. Eating, or overeating makes shopping so dicey, look at my wardrobe with three different sizes hanging there.

After I've shopped, only then I can eat a little, have some of my favourite London treats.

When I'm tired, sugar's good. When I'm unhappy, sugar helps. When I don't like myself, sugar helps. But sugar, my drug of choice, is always bad news in the end. Its effect is fleeting, it's pure white and deadly just like real drugs. Sugar is my cocaine.

Some of us eat to live, some of us live to eat.

SOMETIMES, IT'S NOT FAIR

CHAPTER 31

So welcome to my life, although Philip's must be worse when he's in the hands of the Daily Mail.

My mother thought everything they wrote in the Daily Mail was true. She was a true product of her generation, racist and prejudiced. If she was in the hospital and someone of colour approached to care for her, she flinched.

If a doctor approached who wasn't white, she wouldn't recognise them as a doctor.

'I want a real doctor' she could be heard saying.

Simon and my mother had monumental arguments about asylum seekers, it was their favourite Sunday afternoon sport.

But then she had many sports.

For Brandon's bar mitzvah, the £5-million-pound one to be held in the South of France, we were flummoxed, now there's a word, flummoxed for a gift. I mean, what do you buy the 13-year-old who's got everything? We came up with a wonderful idea, after all, let's use the artist in the family for once.

We created a photo album of his dad's life. No, we didn't just stick photos in an album, you know, with those sticky corners you put on, and then the pictures slide and fall out.

No, we were far more sophisticated than that. We plundered my mother's cupboards and found many, many old photos, and every Sunday we would have the photos spread out on the red baize topped billiards table in our dining room, ready to be sorted through and looked at.

We tried to include her in the conversation as we picked and chose. But my mother wasn't impressed, nothing much impressed her.

'Why would Brandon be interested in a load of old photographs?' Why indeed? Heritage? History? Just might turn out to be more interesting than another watch? (He was given eight watches).

So what we did was, or rather what my ex did, was scan the photos, arrange them on a page and each page had a yellowish tinge. It looked so real I almost wanted to peel the photos off the page. It did look very good, and I invented wonderful titles for each page. The older Philip had got, the more he was in the public eye, and I had collected newspaper cuttings, many, many newspaper cuttings.

I had also, interestingly, kept a pair of 'Joan Collins jeans.' Gloria Vanderbilt had come up with putting her embossed signature on the back pocket of jeans, great branding. Now Joan had done it, or rather my brother had put it on Joan's bum'.

My favourite page in the album we gave to Brandon shows a picture of Sir Philip and Lady Tina, in the presence of the Queen. It's a Royal Command performance of 'Bombay Dreams' the musical.

Philip is slightly bowing to the Queen, shaking her hand. On the other side he is holding Tina's hand. I captioned it 'Royalty meets Royalty.'

I did great captions, but that is my favourite.

Philip liked the album so much he phoned me up and said: 'Thank you, what a lovely present.'

I wish I could have framed that!

So as much as the newspapers loved Philip as an entrepreneurial free spirit, they turned on him and despised him.

Quote:

Daily Mail newspaper, September 18, 2016

Sir Shifty no show: Absence of former BHS owner Philip Green leaves a rather large hole in Topshop's London Fashion Week show.

Roly-poly retailer Sir Philip Green always looms large at his London Fashion Week shows for Topshop.

Yesterday, Sir Shifty, who had become a pariah after selling

BHS to a serial bankrupt for £1, was, however, conspicuous by his absence.

BHS has since been put into administration with the loss of 11,000 jobs.

Green, who still has his knighthood, is usually a staple at Topshop's catwalk presentations.

But his vast space on the front row was taken by a trio of blondes, whose unsmiling demeanours gave the impression that they were hostages in a kidnap video.

Model Lottie Moss seemed to be there instead of her half sister Kate, who is something of a muse to the odious Green.

It's unclear why pop star Ellie Goulding, who sang at the Duke and Duchess of Cambridge's wedding reception, felt the need to attend.

Lady Kitty Spencer, the niece of Princess Diana, definitely should have known better.

Super-tanned Green has been spending his summer on his yacht Lionheart, which is estimated to be worth £100 million pounds, and has its own helipad.

Recently emerged pictures showed him dousing himself in copious amounts of champagne at a party off the Greek Island of Mykonos.

But the fashion show's theme was more down to earth, with Topshop targeting ordinary people interested in high street clothes, rather than the fashionista elite.

The retail giant boasted of its achievement in getting fashion from the runway to retail, saying it was leading the 'democratisation' of London Fashion Week.'

Phew, I wish.

Not really, what an eloquent piece of … crap. I was worrying there for a moment it would forget to get back to the basis of the piece, London Fashion Week.

So much assumption, arrogance, and eloquent insults all wrapped up in one article. You non-Daily Mail readers, this was for you, a sample of what you are missing.

Deprecation and rudeness at its best, I feel sorry. Sorry for those trashed, but I am sure, not burned.

Soon after, he was called to parliament to testify to a committee about a shortfall in the pension fund for BHS. MPs banded together in their condemnation, he was considered the` 'evil face of capitalism.' Vilified and crucified.

But mostly he kept quiet and I kept away, sure my commiserations weren't wanted. After all. we're not so much in contact.

But doesn't mean I don't feel bad. So bad, one day I wrote to Tina, an email not really for her eyes but the only place I could send it. Philip doesn't do emails, doesn't use the computer.

'Letter to Frank Field MP' courtesy of Tina.

Dear Frank,

I understand your frustration and upset about matters seemingly we have elected you to deal with.

If I came to you and insulted you, your family, your work prowess, etc., and then said 'Where's the money?'

How would you feel?

Then bullied you some more, wrote stuff in the papers, bombarded the media with insults about you, then said 'Where's the money?'

How would you feel? Would you be inclined to do what is wanted?

I make no judgement on what is right or wrong either about your behaviour or Sir Philip's.

Taunting and goading won't work! Never have.

Don't you get it? The £10 million for his new house does not take away from the pension fund, they are not connected.

I think he just wants to be spoken to with dignity and respect and truthfulness.

Remember how you felt in Tony Blair's government when your ideas and you were rejected? Your anti-immigration looked down on?

Is this merely you trying to recoup your ground, five minutes of fame back?

You have always been extreme, I'm surprised you haven't noticed your lack of popularity and success.

Be here for the BHS pensions, not your glory.'

Sir Philip Green agrees to hand over £363 million from his personal funds to settle the deficit in the pension fund for BHS, previously his business, which he sold for a pound to a former bankrupt, Dominic Chappell.

Guardian newspaper, Tuesday 28, Feb 2017:

> Frank Field says, "I very much welcome this out-of-court settlement, which is an important milestone in gaining justice for BHS pensioners and former workers."

NOT IN THE SCRIPT

CHAPTER 32

Yesterday, I spent a little minute with Michael Caine, Morgan Freeman, Alan Arkin and the beautiful Ann-Margret.

I did. True. They were on a platform in front of me, I was in the audience.

They were talking about their new film 'Going in Style.'

I got to ask them a question. I simpered somewhat.

'Sir Michael, I'm English, may I call you that?'

'Only I'm allowed to call myself that in the mirror and he's a Lord.' He pointed at Alan Arkin.

They are laughing and playful like naughty schoolkids, old, they're young at heart and keeping us all young too with belly-aching laughter.

I've got the microphone, I'm standing to ask a question. But they are still teasing the previous questioner as he retreats to the back.

'Didn't you like us?' asks Morgan Freeman.

We're all laughing.

'Bet you're not going to see the movie.'

Michael interrupts, 'Ma'am you're waiting to ask a question.'

'Come forward, come forward love, he's deaf and I'm half blind,' says Morgan.

After I've greeted Sir Michael I carry on, 'Spike Milligan, a wonderful comedian, you know him (looking at Michael Caine) wrote on his tombstone 'I told you I was ill.' What would you write on yours?'

Alan Arkin jumps in and says: 'Mine is better luck next time.'

Michael says: 'See you later, no hurry.'

Morgan Freeman says 'Roadkill.' (big laughter)

And when they finally let Ann-Margret speak, she says: 'I tried.'

Morgan Freeman leans forward and says to me, 'What's yours, love?'

For a moment I'm stumped, then I remember the whole reason I ever came up with this phrase.

'Mine's "Not in the Script".'

Sir Michael says, 'I might change mine to that.'

They banter some more then it's over, and I'm left remembering where 'Not in the Script' came from.

It's Philip's 50th birthday party. We took off from Luton Airport. The departure board said 'Undisclosed Destination.'

Even the carpet in the airport lounge was embossed with a PG logo. We were all agog.

My mother was there with Phyllis, her closest friend. There were about 200 of us drinking champagne in the special departure lounge. A few musicians are giving us a little soothing jazz music. My kids are not invited, so it's just me and the grumpy spouse. I'm nervous, and he doesn't care, in fact he's rather reveling in my discomfort. But then, unknown to me, we're getting near the end of the relationship, although if I'd looked harder I would have known. Maybe I just didn't want to look too hard.

Tina's daughter, Stasha, is here. She's just cut the cord from hubby, coming bravely to the party alone.

I'm already feeling underdressed and I don't have a diamond to my name. Never mind, they get unvarnished me! Of course I shopped, prinked, pouted. Nails, hair were as perfect as I could manage. You know there are jeans, and then, there are, JEANS. I'm of course wearing best Topshop, I'm in a minority.

It's a blur of people, many I know. But I'm nervous, waiting to be pounced on by my brother. I chance it and go to say` hi.'

'If you're nice I'll introduce you to people.'

This is the only time over the four days I talk to him. But then I can do my own introductions easy, after all, I'm well-connected.

'Hi, I'm Philip's sister, how are you?'

Most people out of respect for Philip give me a rapturous reception, but mostly I'm stuck with David.

Once on board, there's a buzz, everybody's trying to figure out where we're flying to, and it's obvious Chloe, my niece, knows. But she's not saying. We all, if we followed instructions, have hot weather clothes, and cool for evening.

We mingle on board, eat and drink, the party has started already.

We land in Cyprus in the evening, and four days of celebration begin.

We are treated to George Benson, Tom Jones, and Earth Wind and Fire for starters. Divine. Our table in the ballroom is near the kitchen, that's where we're seated for most of the formal events. This won't be the last time. We have our first brunch on the terrace, the sun shines and the lobby is bedecked with candles and flowers.

People who know the place are sure Tina has put more of everything into the mix.

'There's not usually this many candles or flowers,' say the fancy people who've been to this posh spa before. Me? I'm just drinking it all in.

On the Saturday Tina springs a surprise on the birthday boy. She has organised a 'This is Your Life' presentation with Michael Aspel. He is carrying a big blue book - TV use red - and we're all summoned to the ballroom.

For a moment, I forget the strain of being where I'm not really welcomed or wanted. I run into the ballroom, excited.

At the front of the room is a screen with Philip's picture beamed on to it. There will be guests, some secretly flown in by Tina to surprise him, we'll all be waiting for the surprises.

In front of the screen are two rows of chairs facing the audience, these are obviously for the people taking part. My mother is sitting in the front corner chair holding a sheaf of papers.

'Where do I sit?' I ask breathlessly.

She looks up and sees me, and says, 'Oh, you're not in the script.'

WHAT? There's a phrase to stick in my mind or was it my gut?

After making a fuss I get a seat near her, on condition I keep quiet. Julian the party planner organises it. I demand one for David. Let's see if he can muster some moral support.

We sit squeezed in together. At one point they screen a greeting from my kids. I knew they made the video, just didn't know what it was for, now it all makes sense.

After the fabulous toga night with Rod Stewart, we all fly back to reality, to London, some to Monte Carlo, Vivian and Colin to LA, this is of course the international jet set.

I have plans to go skiing and my flight leaves early in the morning. So when I get home, it's barely worth undressing and lying down. But I do. It's the first time I'm going skiing, I feel past my physical prime, but it's time I tackled skiing.

We're a group of 30 in gorgeous Italy. I immediately fall in love with my handsome young ski instructor, who takes me up on the ski lift, high into the mountains. From the Italian mountain top we can see Austria.

Only problem: we have to get down again, and the plan is to ski. But I know he has thighs of steel so I'm not afraid, just a little daunted and it's a long way down. No wonder they invented these wonderful drinks. I have discovered Bombardino, a hot alpine drink with eggnog-like liqueur, whisky or brandy and whipped cream. It's the best. Almost worth skiing all that way down for.

Almost.

I'm shaking at the bottom, bring on the Bombardinos. Plural.

It's girls' night. I'm not loving being a girl on this trip, they're bitchy and mean and cliquey and … did I mention mean? They want to coach me, I'm resisting.

Finally, someone starts a fun conversation. About headstones. Turns out it's fun, and funny. People are both cute and inventive. Someone says, 'Spike Milligan had on his headstone "I told you I was ill".'

So we're all going to choose what we will have on ours. People know I've just come from the big fancy birthday party, but I haven't really discussed it with anyone.

It's my turn, I'm scratching my head, suddenly I speak up. 'My headstone will say: 'NOT IN THE SCRIPT.'

This has stuck, I have never wavered. I forgive her, but, story of my life.

It fits so perfectly, so no, Sir Michael Caine, you cannot steal it. It's mine.

About the Author

Elizabeth was born in Croydon, Surrey in 'olden times' as her kids refer to them and moved to claim her Jewish identity to Hampstead Garden Suburb, North London, when she was eight years old.

She went to South Hampstead High School, that bastion of female-only strength where her daughter attended decades later. Her daughter fared better.

She fled her first teaching job in North London and went to sit at the feet of her guru in India. She found out later he was the 'free love' guru. She was there for two wonderful years in the late '70s.

Back in London with a ring in her nose, she discovered homeopathy, something she follows to this day.

Married in 1983, divorced in 2007, she did her time, created her best creation, her three wonderful children, and post-divorce, went to New York City to discover who she was.

She owns a restaurant in the West Village in Manhattan, previously called Seabird, now called Planted, which offers delicious plant-based food.

She began writing this book in 2017, the year she was banned from her restaurant by one of her partners, but that's going to be her next book.

Elizabeth loves New York. This is her first long-awaited book, awaited by her!

Printed in Great Britain
by Amazon